etz

The Silent Shades of Sorrow

The Silent Shades of Sorrow

Healing for the Wounded

C. H. SPURGEON
COMPILED BY ZACK ESWINE

CHRISTIAN
HERITAGE

Scripture quotations are based on the *King James Version*.

Some Scripture quotations taken directly from Spurgeon's writings reflect the *King James Version* but are worded slightly differently. They have been left as Spurgeon wrote them.

Zack Eswine is Lead Pastor of Riverside Church, St. Louis, Missouri. He also wrote *Kindled Fire: How the methods of C.H. Spurgeon can help your preaching* (ISBN 978-1-84550-117-4) and *Spurgeon's Sorrows: Realistic Hope for those who Suffer from Depression* (ISBN 978-1-78191-538-7).

Copyright © Zack Eswine 2015

paperback ISBN 978-1-78191-585-1
epub ISBN 978-1-78191-674-2
mobi ISBN 978-1-78191-675-9

10 9 8 7 6 5 4 3 2 1

Published in 2015
in the
Christian Heritage Imprint
of
Christian Focus Publications Ltd,
Geanies House, Fearn, Ross-shire,
IV20 1TW, Scotland, UK.
www.christianfocus.com

Cover design by Daniel van Straaten

Printed and bound by
Bell and Bain, Glasgow

CONTENTS

For Jessica, Nate, Abigail and Caleb

Introduction

"I feel very timid. My illness leaves one half frightened. I am a poor creature. Pray for me."[1]

Pastor Charles Spurgeon was a friend to those who physically and mentally suffered. He and his own dear wife, Susannah, suffered truly through years of physical and mental pains.

In this light, Charles preached transparently about sorrows and their many kinds, including depression in all of its forms. He was no trite preacher. He spoke as one who had been there.

---

1. Charles Spurgeon, *Letters of Charles Haddon Spurgeon* (Edinburgh: Banner of Truth, 1992), 171.

Perhaps because he so sorely needed God's comfort for himself, Charles dug deep for a robust biblical pathway for his sufferings. He found in Jesus, not only a savior, but a fellow-friend for the sorrowing. Over time, out of his own heartbroken miseries, he learned how to sustain with a word him who is weary (Isa. 50:4). He comforted others out of the comfort that he himself had received (2 Cor. 1:4).

This small collection of sermons offers a small but healing taste of Charles Spurgeon's larger body of writing and preaching for our sorrows.[2] I've introduced subheadings, not in the original, to aid the reader. As you read, remember that this pastor understood depression as having three individual or collaborative causes— biological, circumstantial and spiritual. It will help you if you are suffering to keep these categories in mind. Remember too, that in one or two of these sermons, for a few paragraphs, Charles will take a moment to speak harder words. These harder words are not for you who are broken hearted in your various humbled miseries as longing for comfort in Jesus. Instead, these few harder words are aimed at those who might be listening to the preacher but whose hearts had hardened.

In fact, I can introduce this pastor's abiding heart for the sorrowing no better than inviting you to read his own words. If you read right now as one who suffers sorrows and depression, take heart, this pastor defends you.

It is the duty of all men to be careful of the sons of sorrow. There be some who from their very birth are

---

2.   See Zack Eswine, *Spurgeon's Sorrows: Realistic Hope for those who Suffer from Depression* (Scotland, U.K.: Christian Focus, 2014).

marked by melancholy as her own. The silent shades of sorrow are their congenial haunts; the glades of the forest of grief are the only places where their leaf can flourish. Others there are who through some crushing misfortune are brought so low that they never hold up their heads again, but go from that time forth mourning to their graves. Some there be, again, who disappointed in their early youth, either in some fond object of their affections, or else in some project of their young ambition, never can dare to face the world, but shrink from contact with their fellows, even as the sensitive plant curls up its tendrils at the touch. In all flocks there must be lambs, and weak and wounded sheep; and among the flock of men, it seems that there must necessarily be some who should more than others prove the truth of Job's declaration, "man is born to trouble even as the sparks fly upward" (Job 5:7) ...

Alas, it is not every man that has learned this lesson. There are some who deal with others with rough-handed thoughtlessness. "Ah," they say, "if such a one be so foolish as to be sensitive let him be." O speak not thus; to be sensitive, timid, and desponding, is ill enough in itself, without our being hard and untender towards those who are so afflicted. Go forth, and do to others as you would have them do to you; and as you would that others in your hours of despondency would deal with you tenderly and comfortably, so deal tenderly and comfortably with them ...

For although religion changes the moral temperament of men, it does not change the physical. A man who is weak in health before conversion will probably be as weak afterwards, and many a spirit that has a tendency to despondency, has exhibited that tendency after conversion.

We do not profess that the religion of Christ will so thoroughly change a man as to take away from him all his natural tendencies; it will give the despairing something that will alleviate that despondency, but as long as that is caused by a low state of body, or a diseased mind, we do not profess that the religion of Christ will totally remove it.

No, rather, we do see every day that amongst the best of God's servants, there are those who are always doubting, always looking to the dark side of every providence, who look at the threatening more than at the promise, are ready to write bitter things against themselves, and often put the bitter for sweet, and the sweet for bitter, erring against their own spirits and robbing themselves of comforts which they might enjoy.[3]

Among the many and silent shades of sorrow, the sorrowing have a Savior. There is hope for the broken-hearted.

Zack Eswine
Webster Groves, Missouri
April, 2015

---

3. Charles Spurgeon, Sermon 243 Delivered on Sabbath Morning, March 20th, 1859, the Music Hall, Royal Surrey Gardens. http:/ www.spurgeon.org/sermons/0243.htm

1

A Frail Leaf [1]

"Will You break a leaf driven to and fro?"
(Job 13:25)

Poor Job! Who could have been brought lower than he? He had lost his possessions, his children, his health—he was covered with sore boils—and he was aggravated by the unkind speeches of his friends. In his deep distress he turns to God and finding no other plea so near at hand, he makes a plea out of his own distress. He compares himself to the weakest thing he could think of and then he says to

---

1.   Charles Spurgeon, *Metropolitan Tabernacle Pulpit,* Vol. 57. Sermon No. 3269, http://www.spurgeongems.org/vols55-57/chs3269.pdf (accessed March 9, 2015).

God, the Great and the Merciful, "Will You, so glorious in power and so matchless in goodness—will You break me, who am like a poor leaf fallen from the tree, sere and dry, and driven to and fro in the wind?" Thus he draws an argument out of his own weakness. Because he is so low and insignificant and powerless, he lays hold upon the Divine strength and pleads for pity.

Pleading for Pity

It is a common figure he uses, that of a leaf driven to and fro. Strong gusts of wind, it may be in the autumn when the leaves hang but lightly upon the trees, send them falling in showers around us. Quite helpless to stay their own course, fluttering in the air to and fro, like winged birds that cannot steer themselves, but are guided by every fitful blast that blows upon them, at last they sink into the mire to be trodden down and forgotten. To them Job likens himself—a helpless, hopeless, worthless, weak, despised, perishing thing—and he appeals to the awful Majesty on High and he says to the God of thunder and of lightning, "Will You put out Your power to destroy me? Will You bring forth Your dread artillery to crush such an insignificant creature as I am? With all the goodness of Your great heart—for your name is God That Is Good— will You turn Your Almighty power against me? Oh, be that far from You! Out of pity upon my utter weakness and nothingness, turn away Your hands and break not a leaf that is driven to and fro!"

The apprehension is so startling, the appeal so forcible that the argument may be employed in a great many ways. How often have the sick used it, when they have been brought to so low an ebb with physical pain that life, itself, seemed worthless? Stricken with disease, stung with smart and fretted with acute pains and pangs, they feel that if the affliction continues much longer, it were better for them to die then live! They long for the shades of death, that they might find shelter there. Turning their face to the wall, they have said, "O God, as weak as I am, will You again smite me? Shall Your hand again fall upon me? You have laid me very low. Why do You lift up Your rod again? Break not, I beseech You, a leaf that is driven to and fro!"

Not less applicable is the plea to those who are plunged into the depths of poverty! A man is in trouble arising from destitution. Perhaps he has been long out of work. Bread is not to be found. The children are crying, hungry, starving! The habitation has been stripped of everything which might procure a little nourishment. The poor wretch, after passing through seas of trouble, finds himself no nearer a landing place than before, but—

> "Sees each day new straits attend,
> And wonders where the scene will end."[2]

Passing through the streets he is hardly able to keep his feet from the pavement or his skin from the cold by reason of his tattered garments. Homeless and friendless, like a leaf that is driven to and fro, he say, "O God! Will You continue this much longer? Will You not be pleased to stop Your rough wind, mitigate the sharpness of the winter, ease my adversity and give me peace?"

So, too, with those who are in trouble through bereavement. One child has been taken away and then another.

---

2. John Fawcett, "Thus Far My God Has Led Me On," *A Selection of Hymns for the Use of Baptist Congregations* (London: J. Haddon, 1845), 245.

The shafts of death flew twice. Then came sickness with threatening omen upon one that was still nearer and dearer. Still did not the desolation stay its gloomy portents. It seemed at length as though the widow would be bereft of her last and only child and then she cried, "O God! I am already broken. My heart is like a plowed field—cross-plowed—till my soul is ready to despair! Will You utterly break me? Will You spare me no consolations, no props for my old age? Must I be altogether driven away before the whirlwind and find no rest?"

Pity for our Mental Distress

Perhaps it is even more harassing in cases of mental distress for, after all, the sharpest pangs we feel are not those of the body, nor those of the estate, but those of the mind. When the iron enters into the soul, the rust thereof is poison. "The spirit of a man will sustain his infirmity, but a wounded spirit who can bear?"

You may be surrounded with all the comforts of life and yet be in wretchedness more gloomy than death if the spirits are depressed. You may have no outward cause whatever for sorrow and yet if the mind is dejected, the brightest sunshine will not relieve your gloom. At such a time, you may be vexed with cares, haunted with dread and scared with thoughts which distract you. You fear that your sins are not pardoned, that your past transgressions are all brought to remembrance and that punishment is being meted out to you in full measure. The threats rise up out of God's Book and seem to lift sharp swords in their hands with which to smite you. Time is dreadful to you because you know it is hurrying you to eternity—and the thought of eternity stings as does an adder because you measure the future reckoning by the present distress. At such a time, when you are faint with longing, ready to despair and driven to the verge of madness, I can imagine your crying out, "O Lord God of Mercy, I am as a leaf that is driven to and fro—will You quite break me and utterly destroy me? Have compassion, and show Your favor to Your poor broken creature!"

Many a child of God may have used this, and if he has not used it yet, he may still use it. There are times when all our evidences get clouded and all our joys are fled. Though we may still cling to the Cross, yet it is with a desperate grasp. God brings our sins to remembrance till our bones, as David puts it, "are sorely broken by reason of our iniquity." Then it is that, all broken, we can turn to the Strong for strength and use the plea of the text, "Will You break a leaf driven to and fro?" And we shall get for our answer these comforting words, "A bruised reed He will not break, and smoking flax He will not quench" (Isa. 42:3).

Confessing Our Inner Turmoil

What plea is more powerful to ourselves than that which we draw from ourselves? A man may not be sure of anything outside him, for eyes and ears may deceive—but he is always pretty well assured of anything within him, for that which he perceives in his own consciousness he is very tenacious about.

Now, in this case, Job was quite certain about his own weakness. How could he doubt that? He looked upon his poor body covered with sores. He looked upon his friends who had perplexed and vexed him so much and he felt that he was, indeed, just like a sere leaf. I trust that many of us have been brought by God the Holy Spirit into such a humble frame of mind as to feel that, in a certain sense, this is true of us. O God, if we know ourselves right, we are all like withered leaves! We once thought ourselves fresh and green—we reckoned that we were as good as others, we made a fine and verdant profession—but, lo, You have been pleased to deal with us and all the fresh verdure of what we thought to be our piety—the natural piety which we thought we possessed—has faded and withered and now we are convinced that we are altogether as an unclean thing, and that all our righteousnesses are as filthy rags!

No, the hope that we clung to as the leaf clings to the tree, we have had to give up. We are blown away from that. We were once upon the tree of good works—we seemed as if we had life and would always be happy there, but the winds have taken us away and we cannot hold on to our frail hope. We once thought that we could do everything— we now perceive that without Christ we can do nothing! We are cast forth as a branch separated from the vine—we are withered! What can a leaf do? What power has it to resist the wind? Just so we feel now—we can do nothing— even the sin that dwells in us, like the wind, carries us away and we are like the leaf in the wind, subject to its power.

O my Brothers and Sisters, what a great blessing it is to be made to know our own weakness! To empty the sinner of his folly, his vanity and conceit is no easy matter. Christ can easily fill him with wisdom and prudence, but to get him empty—this is the work! This is the difficulty. To make a man know that he is in himself utterly lost, ruined, and undone—this is the Spirit of God's own work!

We ministers cannot make a man see that, however diligently we may point it out. Only the Spirit of God can enlighten the heart to discern it and yet, until a man does see it, he cannot enter into the Kingdom of Heaven, for there are none within the pearly gates who were not once brokenhearted sinners! Who could possibly come there and sing, "Unto Him who loved us, and washed us from our sins in His own blood" (Rev. 1:5) but those who once said, "Pardon my iniquity, for it is great" (Ps. 25:11).

While it is a confession of weakness, it is also an acknowledgment of God's power to push that weakness to a direful conclusion. "Will You break me?" says the text—"Lord, You can do it. In one minute You could take away hope from every one of us now in this House of Prayer." Some there are who are in the house of doom, where prayer can never be answered, and where Mercy's proclamation can never be heard! God could break us. It is an easy thing for Him to destroy! And more, He is not only able, but He has the right to do it if He will, for we are such worthless creatures through our disobedience that we may say, in the words of the hymn—

> "If my soul were sent to Hell,
> Thy righteous law approves it well."[3]

When we feel this, then let us make a proper use of our own consciousness, not to despond and faint, but to arise and go to our Father! So we shall come to God and say, "You can destroy me. You may destroy me justly and I cannot resist You. I cannot save myself from Your vengeance, nor can I merit anything at Your hand. I am as weak as water and altogether as perishing a thing as a

---

3. Isaac Watts, "Psalm 51," http://www.ccel.org/ccel/watts/psalmshymns. toc.html (accessed April 7, 2015).

poor withered leaf—but will You destroy me? I plead for pity. Oh, have pity upon me! O God, let Your heart yearn towards me and show me Your great compassion! I have heard that You delight in mercy and as Ben-Hadad of old, with the rope about his neck, went in unto the king and confessed that he deserved to die, so do I confess! And as the king forgave him, even so do You with me—a guilty culprit trembling in Your Presence!—

"Show pity, Lord! O Lord, forgive!
Let a repenting rebel live."[4]

Pleading Our Weaknesses

Though there is weakness, yet there is also power, for weakness is, for the most part, a prevalent plea with those who are strong and good. I trust you could not see on your road home tonight a poor fainting woman, and pass her by. You could not have brought in before your presence a half-starved child who could not drag its weary limbs along without feeling that you must give relief. The mere sight of weakness draws pity. As a certain town was being sacked, one of the rough soldiers is said to have spared a little child, because it said, "Please, Sir, don't kill me, I am so little." The rough warrior felt the urgency of the plea. You may yourselves plead thus with God. "O God, do not destroy me! I deserve it, but oh, I am so little! Turn Your power upon some greater thing and let Your heart move with compassion towards me!"

The plea gathers force when the weakness is confessed. If a man shall have done you some wrong and shall

---

4   Isaac Watts, "Show Pity Lord, O Lord Forgive," http://www.hymntime. com/tch/htm/s/h/o/showpity.htm (accessed April 7, 2015).

come and acknowledge it, and bow down before you and confess it, why, then, you feel that you cannot take him by the throat, but you say, "Rise, I have forgiven you!" When weakness appeals to strength for protection and confession of guilt is relied on as an argument for mercy, those who are good and strong are pretty sure to be moved with compassion.

But, best of all, going from the positive to the comparative, and from the comparative to the superlative, how a confession of weakness touches your heart when it comes from your own child. If your child has been chastised, has confessed his wrong and pleads with you, how you stay your hand! Or, if the child is sick and something is done to it which pains it, if while the operation is being performed he should look you in the face, and say, "Father, spare your child! I can bear no more!" you have already felt more than you can make him feel, forthwith your own tears blind you and you stay your hand. "Like as a father pities his children, even so the Lord pities them that fear Him." If you have faith to bring your weakness before God with the sense of a child towards Him, you surely must prevail. Come, them, you timid trembling children of your Father who is in Heaven, use this plea—"Will You break a leaf that is driven to and fro?"

The plea is rightly addressed when it is addressed to God. As I thought it over, it seemed to me as if I could use it with reference to each Person of the Blessed Trinity in Unity. Looking up to the great Father of our spirits, from whom every good and perfect gift comes down, it seemed to me that out of weakness I could say to Him, "Will You, whose name is Father, will You break a leaf that is driven to and fro? You are the God that made us—will You utterly destroy the earthen vessel which You have fashioned on Your wheel? Your name is 'Preserver of Men.' Will You annihilate us and break us into shivers? Have You not revealed Yourself as delighting in mercy? Are You not the 'Lord God, merciful and gracious, passing by iniquity, transgression and sin'? Have you not said, 'Come, now, and let us reason together; though your sins are as scarlet, they shall be as white as snow; though they are red like crimson, they shall be as wool'? O God, the Father of Heaven, will You break a leaf that is driven to and fro?"

And then, I thought I could address myself to the blessed Son of God who is also our Brother in human flesh, and say to Him, "Will You break—O You 'faithful High Priest, touched with a feeling of our infirmities'— 'bone of our bone, and flesh of our flesh'—Brother of our soul, by whose stripes we are healed—will You break a leaf that is driven to and fro? No, by Your thorn-crowned head and Your bloody sweat, by Your Cross and passion, by Your wounds and by Your death cry, You cannot, will not, be unmerciful and unkind! Surely they who in confidence turn to You and lay hold upon You, shall find that Your strength shall be ready to help—for though Your arm is strong to smite—it is no less strong to save."

Again, it comes across me sweetly, "O blessed Spirit! Could You break a leaf that is driven to and fro? You are no eagle—you did descend on Christ in Jordan as a dove—your influences are soft and soothing. Your name is, 'The Comforter.' You take of the things of Christ, not to blast us, but to bless us therewith. You are not a destroying Spirit, but a quickening Spirit, not a terrifying but an enlivening Spirit—will You break a leaf that is driven to and fro?"

"Yes, I address You, You Triune God, You who are so full of mercy, and love, and Grace, and truth, that those who have known You best have been compelled to say, 'Oh, how great is Your goodness which You have laid up for them that fear You! Oh, the depths of Your loving kindness!' is it possible that You can cast away a poor, broken-hearted trembler, a poor, fearing, doubting one who would gladly be saved, but who trembles lest he should be cast away?"

Stories of Hope

This plea is backed up by many cases of success. We will not give many, for we have not time, but there is one case which we will mention. There was a woman whose life was exceedingly sorrowful. She was an Eastern wife and her husband had been foolish enough to have a second mistress in the house. The woman of whom we speak, a holy woman, a woman of refined and delicate mind, a poetess, indeed, of no mean order—this poor woman, having no children was the constant butt of her rival, whose sneering spiteful remarks chaffed and chafed her. Her adversary, it is said, "vexed her sore to make her afraid." Though her husband was exceedingly kind to her, yet as with a sword that cut her bones did she continually go. She was a woman of a sorrowful spirit, her spirit being broken.

Still, "she feared the Lord exceedingly," and she went up to God's House, and it was in God's House that she received what was to her, perhaps, the greatest blow of her life! If it was from her rival that she received the harshest word, it was from the High Priest of God that she received this hardest blow! As she stood there praying, using no vocal sound, but her lips moving, the High Priest—an easy-going soul who had brought his own family to ruin by his slackness—little knowing her grief, told her that she was drunk! Being a woman to whom the thought of such a sin was as bitter as gall, it must have smitten her as with the chill blast of death, that God's Priest had said she was drunk!

But, as you will all remember, the Lord did not break the leaf that was driven to and fro. There came to her a comfortable promise. Ere long that woman stood there to sing! The mercy of God had made the barren woman to rejoice and to be the joyful mother of children! The song of the Virgin Mary was modeled after the song of Hannah—that memorable poem in which she sang of the Lord who had filled the hungry with good things, while the rich He had sent away empty. In that case the Lord did not break the leaf that was driven to and fro (1 Sam. 1–2)!

In later years—to take an example of another kind—there was a king who had sinned desperately, slaying God's servants with both hands. But he was taken captive by a powerful monarch and thrown into prison—such an offensive prison that he was among thorns—in mental as well as in material darkness. Then, troubled in spirit, tossed to and fro, and without power to help himself, Manasseh sought the Lord and he found the Lord—he prayed unto the Lord and the Lord heard him! Out of the low dungeon He did not break the leaf that was driven to and fro (2 Chron. 33:1-13)!

Take a later case, in our Savior's time. The picture of those proud Pharisees hurrying into our Savior's Presence a poor fallen woman is even now in your mind's eye. Yes, Sirs, she was taken in adultery. There was no doubt of it. She was "taken in the very act," and there she stands—no, she kneels—all covered with blushes before the Man who is asked to judge her! And you remember His words? He never said a word to excuse her guilt—the Savior could not and would not condone her shame! Nor would He, on the other hand, lend Himself to crush the woman who had sinned, but He said—"Where are those, your accusers? Go and sin no more!" Let His words come unto you, poor leaf, driven to and fro! Oh, if there should be such a leaf as that driven here tonight, driven in, perhaps, by stress of weather! Men despise you—from your own sex you get faint pity—but Jesus, when you appeal to Him—will not break such a leaf that is driven to and fro (John. 8:1-11)!

Shall I tell another story of the woman who came behind the Master, in the press, and stole a cure by touching His garment? She thought she would receive a curse, but He said—"Be you of good cheer. Your faith has made you whole. Go in peace." It was poor faith—it was very much like unbelief, but yet it was rewarded with a rich acceptance, for He will not break a leaf that is driven to and fro (Matt. 9:20-22)!

God is Merciful and Bountiful in His Help

Once more, my text is a faint plea which invites full succor. "Will You break a leaf that is driven to and fro?" O Job! There is much wrapped up in what you have said! He meant this—"Instead of breaking it, You will spare it; You will gather it up, You will give it life again." It is like that text, "A bruised reed He will not break" (Isa. 42:3). Oh, it means more than that—it means that He will heal its bruises. "A smoking flax He will not quench." That is good, but it means more! It means that He will stoop down to it and with His soft breath He will blow that smoking flax

25

into a flame—He will not let it go out! He will preserve its heat and make something more of it. O you who are brought to the very lowest of weakness, use that weakness in pleading with God, and He will return unto you with such a fullness of blessing that you shall receive the pardon of sin! You shall be accepted through the righteousness of Christ! You shall be dear to the heart of God! You shall be filled with His Spirit and you shall be blessed with all the fullness of God!

My Lord is such an One that if a beggar asks a penny of Him, He gives him gold! And if you ask only for the pardon of sins, He will give you all the Covenant blessings which He has been pleased so bounteously to provide for the necessities of His people! Come, poor guilty one—needy, helpless, broken and bruised—come by faith and let your weakness plead with God through Jesus Christ!

We may use this plea—many of us who have long known the Savior. Perhaps our faith has got to be very low. O Lord, will You destroy my little faith? I know there is sin in it. To be so unbelieving as I am is no little crime, but Lord, I thank You that I have any faith. It is weak and trembling, but it is faith of Your own giving. Oh, break not the poor leaf that is driven to and fro!

It may be your hope is not very bright. You cannot see the golden gates, though they are very near. Well, but your hope shall not be destroyed because it is clouded. You can say, "Lord, will You destroy my hope because it is dim?" No, that He will not!

Perhaps you are conscious that you have not been as useful, lately, as you once were, but you may say, "Lord, will You destroy my usefulness because I have been laid aside, or have not done what I ought to have done in Your service?" Bring your little Graces to Christ as the mothers brought their little children, and ask Him to put His hands upon them and to bless them. Bring your mustard seed to Christ and ask Him to make it grow into a tree, and He will do it! But never think that He will destroy you, or that He will destroy the works of His own hands in you!

Oh, that I could so preach as to give the comfort to you which I have felt in my own soul while musing over these words! I wish that some who feel how lost, how empty and how ruined they are, could now believe in the great and the good heart of my Lord Jesus Christ. Little do they know how glad He will be to save them. You will be glad to be saved, but He will be more glad to save you. You will be thankful to sit at the feast, but of all that come to the banquet, there is no heart as glad as the heart of the King! When the King came in to see the guests, I know there were gleams of joy in His face which were not to be found in the faces of any of the guests. He has the joy of benevolence!

Perhaps you have sometimes felt a thrill of pleasure when you have done some good to your poor fellow creatures. Now, think what must be the joy of Christ, the joy of the Father and the joy of the Holy Spirit—the joy of doing good to those who do not deserve it, the joy of bestowing favors upon the wicked and the unthankful, the joy of showing that He does good because He is good—not because you are good, but because He is good! Thus the Lord God will leap over the mountains of your sins, your prejudices and the rivers of your iniquities, that He may come unto you and display the full Glory of His loving kindness and His tender mercy! Oh, that some might now for the first time be drawn to Jesus, put their trust in Him and find pardon and peace!

2

Sweet Stimulants for the Fainting Soul[1]

"O my God, my soul is cast down within me:
therefore will I remember You from the land of
Jordan, and of the Hermonites,
from the hill Mizar."
(Psalm 42:6)

Here is a common complaint of God's people and here are two remedies which David, wisely guided of God, administers with discretion. Let us direct our meditation in this order—first, let us talk of the complaint. And then, secondly, let us look into the Divine medicine chest and use the remedies provided there.

---

1.   Charles Spurgeon, *Metropolitan Tabernacle Pulpit,* Vol. 48, Sermon #2798, www.spurgeongems.org (accessed March 9, 2015).

Our Soul's Complaint

First, let us talk of the complaint. "O my God, my soul is cast down within me." We do not know what was the precise reason why David's soul was cast down. Perhaps it was because he had been driven out of the royal city by his own son—the son whom he had petted and pampered and, thereby, made a rod for his own back. We are pretty sure that he was now denied the privilege of going up to the House of God—he could not now join with the multitude that kept holy day. These two things probably worked together to cast down his spirit—his absence from the tabernacle and the cause of that absence.

I am not sure, however, that these two things combined would have been enough to cast down David's spirit if it had not been for a more bitter ingredient in his cup of sadness. There have been good men in circumstances similar to David's at that time who, even then, could gird up the loins of their mind and hope to the end. When bitten by that which is sharper than a serpent's tooth—an ungrateful child—and debarred from the House of God, they have, even then, been able to stay themselves upon the Lord and to rejoice in the Most High God.

The real reason of the Psalmist's distress was, no doubt, that God had, at least to some degree, hidden His face from him and, therefore, the flowers of David's graces all drooped and his joy, which formerly sparkled in the sunlight of God's Countenance, was now dim and dark. Troubles may distress the outward man, but they cannot distress the soul of the child of God while he feels the Lord Jehovah to be his everlasting strength. Yes, it sometimes happens that the very pressure which weighs down the scale of his earthly hopes tends to lift up the opposite scale of his spiritual peace! As long as God is with him, trials are nothing, for he casts them upon Jehovah. But once let God withdraw from him for a while and he is troubled—that mountain which seemed to stand fast begins to rock and shake—and to prove the instability and insufficiency of all mortal grounds of confidence.

Bodily and Circumstantial Causes of Depression

The causes of our being cast down are very numerous. Sometimes it is pain of body—perhaps a wearing pain which tries the nerves, prevents sleep, distracts our attention, drives away comfort and hides contentment from our eyes. Often, too, has it been debility of body—some secret disease has been sapping and undermining the very strength of our life and we knew not that it was there while we have been drawing insensibly near to the gates of death. We have wondered that we were low in spirits, whereas it would have been a thousand wonders if we had not been depressed! We have marveled that we have been cast down, whereas a physician would tell us that this was but one of many symptoms which proved that we were not right as to our bodily health.

Not infrequently has some crushing calamity been the cause of depression of spirit. Trial has succeeded trial. All your hopes have been blasted, your very means of sustenance have been suddenly snatched from you. While all your needs have remained, the supplies have been withdrawn from you.

At other times, it has been bereavement that has brought you down very low. The axe has been at work in the forest of your domestic joys. Tree after tree has fallen— those from whom you plucked the ripest fruits of sweet society and kindred fellowship have been cut down by the ruthless woodsman—you have seen them taken away from you forever so far as this world is concerned.

Or else it may be that you have been slandered. Your good has been evilly spoken of, your holiest motives have been misinterpreted, your most Divine aspirations have been misrepresented and you have gone about as with a sword in your bones while the malicious have taunted you, saying, "Where is your God now?"

The cases of depression of spirit are so various that it must be, indeed, a rare panacea, a marvelous remedy, which would suit them all! Yet, when we come to speak of the remedies mentioned in our text, we shall find them suitable to most of these cases, if not to all—and to all in a degree, if not to the fullest extent.

Spiritual Aspects of Depression

Let us pass now, from the most obvious, to the more subtle causes of soul-dejection. This complaint is very common among God's people. When the young Believer has first to suffer from it, he thinks that he cannot be a child of God, "For," he says, "if I were a child of God, would I be like this?" What fine dreams some of us have when we are just converted! We fancy that we are going to sail straight away to Heaven and to have a prosperous voyage all the way! The wind is always to blow fairly for us, there is never to be a rough wave, no storm-cloud is to hover over the ship all the day long—and if there are any nights, the stars will be so brilliant that it will be as bright as day! Or, possibly, we imagine that we have come into a country where everybody will be kind to us, where all circumstances will be propitious to us, where everything will tend to nurture our piety and our own hearts—indeed, will forever get rid of legal terrors and perilous alarms! Oh, silly creatures that we are if we dream thus foolishly! We know not what we are born to in our second birth, for, as a man is born to trouble by his first birth—when he is born a second time, he is born to a double share of trouble! Then, he was born to physical and mental trouble, but now that he is born-again, he is born to spiritual trouble and as he shall have new joys, so shall he also have a long list of new sorrows.

All that, however, is unknown to us at the first. And when it comes upon us, it surprises us. Am I now addressing one who is ready to exclaim, "I give up all hope. I am sure I cannot be a child of God because I am so cast down"? O you simple soul, the most advanced saints suffer in just the same way! Men who have been for forty, fifty, sixty years followers of Christ complain that, sometimes, it is a question with them whether they have ever known Christ at all! There are seasons with them when they would, if they could, creep into any mouse hole and hide their heads rather than be seen among God's people because they fear that they are hypocrites—and that the root of the matter is not in them. Why, I tell you, young Christians, that the most experienced Believers, the men who have great doctrinal knowledge and much experimental wisdom, the men who have lived very near to God and have had the most rapt and intimate fellowship with their Lord and Savior are the very men who have their ebbs, their winters and their times when it is a moot point with them whether they really love the Lord or not!

Even the Apostle Paul was not exempt from doubts and fears, for he wrote, "We were troubled on every side; without were fightings, within were fears" (2 Cor. 7:5).

And, on another occasion, "I keep under my body, and bring it into subjection: lest that by any means, when I have preached to others, I myself should be a castaway" (1 Cor. 9:27). The man after God's own heart, even David, a man of experience so deep that none of us can fully decipher, much less rival it—a man of love so fervent that few of us can do more than aspire to catch the hallowed flame—nevertheless, had to cry aloud, and that very often, "O my God, my soul is cast down within me!"

"But," says one, "this death-like faintness comes upon me so often that, certainly I cannot be a child of God." Yes, but let me tell you that, possibly, it will come even more! Or, should it come more seldom, if you shall have weeks of pleasure, or even months of enjoyment, it is possible that your doubts will then be doubled in intensity and your soul will yet have greater trials to experience!

So great a Savior is provided for our deliverance that we must expect to have great castings down from which we need to be delivered. Why, Believer, what are one half of the promises worth if we are not the subjects of doubts and fears? Why has Jehovah given us so many shalls and wills but because He knew that we should have so many accursed ifs and perhaps? He would never have given us such a well-filled storehouse of comfort if He had not foreseen that we would have a full measure of sorrow. God never makes greater provision than will be needed, so, as there is an abundance of consolations, we may rest assured that there will also be an abundance of tribulations! There will be much fear and casting down to each of us before we see the face of God in Heaven! This disease of soul-dejection is common to all the saints—there are none of God's people who altogether escape it.

Let me go a step further and say that the disease mentioned in our text, although it is exceedingly painful, is not at all dangerous. When a man has a toothache, it is often very distressing, but it does not kill him. There have been some who have foolishly and peevishly wished to die to escape from the pain, but nobody does die of it. The bills of mortality are not swelled by its victims. And, in like manner, God's children are much vexed with their doubts and fears, but they are never killed by them. They are a great trouble, but they are not like a mortal disease. They are sorely vexatious, but they are not destructive.

The Strange Riddles of our Hearts

Why, it is possible for you to have real faith and yet to have the most grievous unbelief! "Oh," you say, "how can faith and unbelief live together?" They cannot live together in peace, but they may dwell together in the same heart. Remember what our Lord Jesus said to Peter "O you of little faith, why did you doubt? (Matt. 14:31). He did not say, "O you of no faith," but, "of little faith." Thus there was some faith, though there was also much doubt.

So, in the Psalmist, there was some faith—there was, indeed, a great deal of faith—for he said, "O my God," and it takes great faith to truly say, "my God." Yet is there not also great unbelief here? Otherwise, would his soul have been cast down at all? But, meanwhile, had he not the yearnings of lively hope in God? If not, would he have dared to say, "Therefore will I remember You from the land of Jordan, and of the Hermonites, from the Hill Mizar?"

The fact is, we are the strangest mixture of contradictions that ever was known. We shall never be able to understand ourselves. God knows us altogether, but we shall never, at least in this life, completely comprehend ourselves. You remember that verse about the holy women at the sepulcher of Christ? After they had heard the angel's message, "they departed quickly from the sepulchre with fear and great joy" (Matt. 28:8). What a strange mixture! On the one hand, we have the golden fruit of joy—and on the other hand, the black fruit of fear. So it makes a kind of checker-work—there are black pieces and red ones, joys and sorrows, bliss and mourning mingled together! The highest joy and the deepest sorrow may be found in the Christian and the truest faith and yet the most grievous doubts may meet together in the child of God. Of course, they only meet there to make his heart a battlefield—but there they may meet—and his faith may be real while his doubts are grievous.

I would remark, yet further, that it is not only possible for a man to thus be cast down and yet to have true faith all the while, but he may actually be growing in Grace while he is cast down! Yes, and he may really be standing higher when he is cast down than he did when he stood upright. Strange riddle! But we who have passed through this experience know that it is true. When we are flat on our faces, we are generally the nearest to Heaven. When we sink the lowest in our own esteem, we rise the highest in fellowship with Christ and in knowledge of Him. Someone said, "The way to Heaven is not upward, but downward." There is some truth in the saying, though it is upward in Christ, it is downward in self. As Dr. Watts sings—the inverse is equally true—

"The more Your glories strike my eyes,
The humbler I shall lie."[2]

---

2. "Hymn 68," http://www.ccel.org/ccel/watts/psalmshymns.II.68.html (accessed April 4, 2015)

This very casting down into the dust sometimes enables the Christian to bear a blessing from God which he could not have carried if he had been standing upright. There is such a thing as being crushed with a load of Grace—bowed down with a tremendous weight of benedictions—having such blessings from God that if our soul were not cast down by them, they would be the ruin of us. It is a good thing for us, sometimes, when fears frighten us and prosperity distresses us.

Some of you may not understand what I am saying. You will not until you have this experience of which I have been speaking, but it does so happen that bitters often cleanse and sweeten the spiritual palate of God's children, while there are sweets which make their mouth full of bitters! I know that I have had songs in the night after I have had groaning during the day and, often, a salutary blow from God's loving hand, though it has made me smart, has cured me of some other far more baneful smart. Where kisses wounded, blows have healed.

The Christian life is a riddle and most surely are God's people familiar with that riddle in their experience. They must work it out before they can understand it. So I say again that this casting down is consistent with the most elevated degree of piety. Depression of spirit is no index of declining Grace—the very loss of joy and the absence of assurance may be accompanied by the greatest advancement in the spiritual life.

Mark you, if it continues month after month, and even year after year, then it is a sign of great weakness of faith—but if it comes only occasionally, as clouds pass over our sky, it is well. We do not want rain all the days of the week and all the weeks of the year, but if the rain comes sometimes, it makes the fields fertile and fills the brooks—and after the shower has fallen and the sun shines again, it puts a new brightness upon the face of Nature and makes the birds clear their throats and sing a new song! The earth never looks so beautiful as when she rises up like one that has washed his face in the brook and, in the shining water, shows the freshness of her verdure and tells of the wondrous skill with which God has been pleased to adorn her. Even so is it with the Christian when he comes forth from great and sore troubles with his harp returned, his psaltery vocal with praise and his lips gratefully confessing to his God, "You have increased my greatness and comforted me on every side" (Ps. 71:21).

The Painful Benefits of Sorrows in the Soul

Painful as is this disease of soul—dejection—it is often very helpful to our spirit when we are obliged to cry, with David, "O my God, my soul is cast down within me." To be cast down is often the best thing that could happen to us. Do you ask, "Why?" Because, when we are cast down, it checks our pride. We are very apt to grow too big. It is a good thing for us to be taken down a notch or two. We sometimes rise so high, in our own estimation, that unless the Lord took away some of our joy, we would be utterly destroyed by pride. Were it not for this thorn in the flesh, we would be exalted beyond measure.

Besides, when this downcasting comes, it gets us to work at self-examination. That religion which has begun to be a matter of form and ritual to us, becomes a thing to be considered in deeper earnest. We look at it as a real thing because of our real doubts. Often, I am sure, when your house has been made to shake, it has caused you to see whether it was founded upon a rock. While your ship had nothing but fine weather, you sailed along too presumptuously. But when the storm threatened, then it was that you reefed your sails and turned to your chart to find your latitude and longitude, fearing that there might be danger ahead. So you get good to your soul by being made to examine yourself.

A great loss in business has sometimes helped a man to become rich, for he has been more careful in his dealings afterwards. He has begun to change a system of trade which, perhaps, might have brought him to insolvency—and thus his business has been put upon a firmer footing than before. Even so, this downcasting of spirit, by leading us to search ourselves, may help, in the end, to make us all the richer in Divine Grace.

When our soul is cast down within us we begin to have closer dealings with Christ than we had before. A long continuance of calm induces listlessness. There is a way of being wanton towards Christ. We begin to think that we can do without Him—we imagine that we have such a store of ready money that we can trade on our own account. But when gloomy doubts arise, we go back to the place where our spiritual life commenced and we sing again—

"Nothing in my hand I bring,
simply to Your Cross I cling."[3]

There is such a tendency in all the branches of the living and true Vine to try to bring forth fruit without deriving nourishment from the stem, so the Lord, every now and

---

3. August Toplady, "Rock of Ages," (1776) http://www.cyberhymnal.org/htm/r/o/rockages.htm (accessed April 4, 2015)

then, takes away the visible flowing of Divine consolation in order that we may consciously realize our entire dependence upon Him.

When you and I were little and we were out at eventide walking with our father, we sometimes used to run on a long way ahead, but, by-and-by, there was a big dog loose on the road and it is astonishing how closely we then clung to our father! You remember how John Bunyan depicts that trait in the character of the children who went on pilgrimage with their mother, Christiana. "When they were come up to the place where the lions were, the boys that went before were glad to cringe behind, for they were afraid of the lions and so they stepped back and went behind. At this their guide smiled and said, 'How now, my boys, do you love to go before when no danger does approach, and love to come behind as soon as the lions appear?'"[4]

Just so is it with our doubts and fears. We run so far ahead that we lose sight of Christ—frightful things alarm us—and then we flee back again to the shadow of His Cross! This experience is good and healthful for us.

One other benefit that we derive from being cast down is that it qualifies us to sympathize with others. If we had never been in trouble we would be very poor comforters of others. It would do most physicians good if they were required, occasionally, to drink some of their own medicine. It would be no disadvantage to a surgeon if he once knew what it was to have a broken bone. You may depend upon it that his touch would be more tender afterwards! He would not be so rough with his patients as he might have been if he had never felt such pain himself.

---

4.   John Buynan, *Pilgrim's Progress.*

Show me a man who has never had a trial and I will show you a man who has no heart. Above all things, save me from the man who has never had any trouble all his life—let me not go into his house, or be near him anywhere else. If I am sick, let him not even pass by my window lest his shadow should fall upon me and make me worse, for he must be a cold-hearted, unsympathetic man if he has never known a trial and has never had to pass through the furnace of affliction!

A Word to Ministers

I know that whenever God chooses a man for the ministry and means to make him useful, if that man hopes to have an easy life of it, he will be the most disappointed mortal in the world! From the day when God calls him to be one of His captains and says to him, "See, I have made you to be a leader of the hosts of Israel," (2 Sam. 7:8), he must accept all that his commission includes—even if that involves a sevenfold measure of abuse, misrepresentation and slander. We need greater soul-exercise than any of our flock, or else we shall not keep ahead of them. We shall not be able to teach others unless God thus teaches us. We must have fellowship with Christ in suffering as well a fellowship in faith.

Still, with all its draw-backs, it is a blessed service and we would not retire from it. Did we not accept all this with our commission? Then we would be cowards and deserters if we were to turn back! These castings down of the spirit are part of our calling! If you are to be a good soldier of Jesus Christ, you must endure hardness. You will have to lie in the trenches, sometimes, with a bullet lodged here or there, with a saber cut on your forehead, or an arm or a leg

shot away—where there is war, there must be wounds—
and there must be war where there is to be victory!

The Consolations of Grace

I shall not say more about our being cast down. I have
probably said enough about the disease, so now let us open
the great medicine chest, and examine the two remedies
here mentioned. "O my God, my soul is cast down within
me: therefore will I remember You from the land of Jordan,
and of the Hermonites, and from the Hill Mizar."

The first remedy for soul-dejection is, a reference of
ourselves to God, as David says, "O my God, my soul is
cast down within me: therefore will I remember You." If
you have a trouble to bear, the best thing for you to do is
not to try to bear it at all, but to cast it upon the shoulders
of the Eternal! If you have anything that perplexes you,
the simplest plan for you will be not to try to solve the difficulty, but to seek direction from Heaven concerning it.
If you have, at this moment, some doubt that is troubling
you, your wisest plan will be not to combat the doubt, but
to come to Christ just as you are and to refer the doubt
to Him.

Remember how men act when they are concerned in a
lawsuit—if they are wise, they do not undertake the case
themselves. They know our familiar proverb, "He who is
his own lawyer has a fool for his client." So they take their
case to someone who is able to deal with it and leave it
with him. Well, now, if men have not sufficient skill to
deal with matters that come before our courts of law,
do you think that you have skill enough to plead in the
court of Heaven against such a cunning old attorney as
the devil who has earned the name of "the accuser of the

brethren," and well deserves the title? Never try to plead against him, but put your case into the hands of our great Advocate, for, "if any man sin, we have an advocate with the Father, Jesus Christ the righteous" (1 John 2:1). So, refer your case to Him—He will plead for you and win the day! If you should attempt to plead for yourself, it will cause you a vast amount of trouble and then you will lose the day after all.

Often, when I call to see a troubled Christian, do you know what he is almost sure to say? "Oh, Sir, I do not feel this—and I do fear that—and I cannot help thinking the other!" That great "I" is the root of all our sorrows— what I feel, or what I do not feel—that is enough to make anyone miserable! It is a wise plan to say to such an one, "Oh, yes! I know that all you say about yourself is only too true, but, now, let me hear what you have to say about Christ. For the next twenty four hours at least, leave off thinking about yourself and think only of Christ." O my dear Friends, what a change would come over our spirits if we were all to act thus! For when we have done with self and cast all our cares upon Christ, there remains no reason for us to care, or trouble, or fret! That saying of Jack the Huckster, which I have often repeated—"I'm a poor sinner, and nothing at all, But Jesus Christ is my All-in-All"[5]—describes the highest experience, though it is also the lowest.

It is so simple and yet so safe, to live day by day by faith upon the Son of God who loved me, and gave Himself for me—to be a little child—not a strong man, but a little

---

5. See for example, G.S. Bowes, *Illustrative Gatherings for Preachers and Teachers* (Philadelphia: Perkinpine and Higgins, 1864), 27.

child who cannot fight his own battles, but who gets Jesus to fight them for him! To be a little weak one who cannot run alone, but who must be carried in the arms of the Good Shepherd. We are never so strong as when we are weak, as Paul wrote, "When I am weak, then am I strong" (2 Cor. 12:10). And we are never so weak as when we are strong, never so foolish as when we are wise in our own conceit and never so dark as when we think we are full of the Light of God. We are generally best when we think we are worst! When we are empty, we are full—when we are full, we are empty. When we have nothing, we have all things, but when we fancy that we are "rich and increased with goods, and have need of nothing," we are like the Laodiceans and know not that we are "wretched, and miserable, and poor, and blind, and naked" (Rev. 3:17). Oh, for Grace to solve these riddles and so to live, day by day, out of self and upon the Lord Jesus Christ!

Taking Hold of God's Promises

Let me give you an illustration. It is the easily-imagined case of a poor old woman who has no money of her own, but who has a rich friend who says to her, "Come to my house every Saturday and I will give you so much for a regular allowance. And if there is anything else that you need, I will pay for it—all your needs shall be supplied." He does not give her a large sum of money to keep, for she might not know how to spend it wisely, or she might be robbed of it—he gives it to her week by week. One Saturday morning the old lady is full of fear and alarm. If you happen to call upon her just then, you will hear her complaining, "I have not a farthing in the world! I have just spent my last sixpence. I have no money in the bank, no houses from which I can collect rent! I have nothing but these few things that you see here—how am I to live with only this?" If you did not know anything more about the woman, you would sit down and pity her, would you not?

As it gets to be nearly twelve o' clock, she says, "I must be going." You ask, "Where?" She replies, "I am going to my friend who tells me to go to him every Saturday and he will give me all I need." "Why," you exclaim, "you silly old soul, you have been telling me all this tale of need and exciting my pity, when you are really a rich woman! Just because you do not happen to have it in hand, you have been telling me this pitiful story which is really not true."

In like manner, when I see an heir of Heaven sitting down and mourning and weeping because he has not got this, and he has not got that—and when I turn to the Scriptures, and read, "... all are yours; and you are Christ's, and Christ is God's" (1 Cor. 3:22-23). And I find promises like this, "All things, whatever you shall ask in prayer, believing, you shall receive" (Matt. 21:22). Or this, "The LORD God is a sun and shield: the LORD will give grace and glory: no good thing will He withhold from them that walk uprightly" (Ps. 84:11).

If I do not say this to the one who is murmuring without cause, I say it to myself, for I have often been as foolish as the old woman of whom I spoke just now, "O you foolish self, how slow of heart you are to believe! How foolish you are to be thus sitting down and bemoaning your own emptiness when Christ is yours, with all His boundless fullness, when the Father's love and the Spirit's power and the Savior's Grace are all engaged to bring you safely through your trials, to rid you of your troubles and to land you triumphantly in Heaven!" Be of good cheer, then, tried and depressed Believer, and apply this sacred remedy to yourself! Remember the Lord! Refer your case to Him and look to Him for all that you need!

Taking Hold of Past Mercies

David's other remedy for his soul, when it was cast down within him, was the grateful remembrance of the past when, by the Lord's tender mercies, it was lifted up— "therefore will I remember You from the land of Jordan, and of the Hermonites, from the Hill Mizar."

Look up your old diary—many of you have gray hair— so your notebooks go back a long way. Let us read one or two of the entries. Why, here is a bright page! Though the one preceding it is black and full of sorrow, this page is bright with joy and jubilant with song! What do I read? I see written here—

> "I will praise Thee every day
> Now Thine anger's turn'd away;
> Comfortable thoughts arise
> From the bleeding sacrifice."[6]

You wrote that verse in your diary just after you had found the Savior and your sins had been forgiven you for His sake. Well, then, although your harp is now unstrung and you are not praising your Lord today, I pray you to remember that hour when first you knew His love and to say, "If I had never received more than that one mercy from Him, I must bless Him for it in time and bless Him for it throughout eternity!"

---

6. William Cowper, "I will praise Thee every day," *Olney Hymns* http://www.theotherpages.org/poems/olney01.html (Accessed April 4, 2015).

Here is another page in your diary. I see that you had been enduring some temporal trouble and that your earthly friends had forsaken you. But, in the middle of your trouble, just where I might have expected to find these words, "I am utterly cast down, for God has forsaken me," I find written here—

> "When trouble, like a gloomy cloud
> Has gathered thick and thundered loud,
> He near my soul has always stood,
> His loving kindness, oh, how good!"[7]

Do you think that He is not standing by your side now? If there is a loud thundering and if there is a thick darkness, will He leave you? Surely these reflections upon what you have experienced in the past should lead you to trust in Christ for the present! And, as you think of all His dealings with your soul, You may well say—

> "Can He have taught me to trust in His name,
> And thus far have brought me to put me to shame?"[8]

God forbid that we should ever think that He was so cruel as to enlighten, comfort, cheer and help us so long and then leave us, at last, to sink and perish!

In this diary of yours, I also find one sweet record which is a great contrast to your present sad and gloomy

7. Samuel Medley, "Loving Kindness," *The People's Hymnbook: A Selection of the Most Popular Psalms, Hymns and Spiritual Songs* by Samuel Shieffelin (Philadelphia: The American Sunday School Union, 1839), 15. https://books.google.com/books (accessed April 4, 2015).

8. John Newton, "I Will Trust and Not Be Afraid," Hymn XXXVII, *Olney Hymns*.

state. You must have had a vision of Christ Crucified, for you have written—

> Here I'll sit forever viewing
> Mercy's streams, in streams of blood.
> Precious drops! My soul bedewing,
> Plead and claim my peace with God.
> Truly blessed is this station,
> Low before His Cross to lie—
> While I see Divine compassion
> Floating in His languid eyes.[9]

Yet you, who have been at the foot of the Cross, are afraid that you will be cast away at the last! You have known the sweetness of Jesus' love, yet you are cast down! He has kissed you with the kisses of His lips—His left hand has been under your head and His right hand has embraced you—yet you think He will leave you to sink, at last, in your trouble! You have been in His banqueting house and you have had such food as angels never tasted, yet you dream that you shall be cast into Hell! Shame on you! Pluck off those robes of mourning! Lay aside that sackcloth and those ashes! Snatch your harps down from the willows and let us together sing praises unto Him whose love, power, faithfulness and goodness shall always be the same!

If there are any here who are strangers to all these things, I can only wish that they might even know our sorrows, in order that they might have an experience of our joys to treasure up in remembrance. Believers in Jesus are not a miserable crew—they have songs to sing and they have good reason to sing them! They have enough to make them blessed on earth and to make them blessed forever and ever!

---

9.   http://www.stempublishing.com

3

Faintness and Refreshing[1]

*"And he arose, and did eat and drink, and went
in the strength of that meat forty days and forty
nights unto Horeb the mount of God."*
(1 Kings 19:8)

Our Fainting Fits

My first observation upon this passage is that the greatest
believers are sometimes subject to fainting fits.

The Apostle James tells us that "Elijah was a man
subject to like passions as we are" (James 5:17). And this
fact was very clearly manifest on the occasion to which
our text refers. Otherwise he seemed, in most things, to
be superior to the ordinary run of men, a sort of iron

---

1. Charles Spurgeon, *Metropolitan Tabernacle Pulpit,* Vol. 54, Sermon
    #3110, Volume 54 www.spurgeongems.org (accessed March 9, 2015).

Prophet—what if I call him the Prophet of Fire—the man whose whole life seemed to be a flash of flame—a mighty, burning, ecstatic love and zeal towards the cause of God?

But Elijah had his flaws, even as the sun has its spots. Strong man though he was, he was sometimes obliged to faint, even as the sun sometimes suffers an eclipse. His fainting, too, took a form which is very common among the saints of God. He cried, "O LORD, take away my life; for I am not better than my fathers" (1 Kings 19:4). A desire to depart, when it arises from wisdom and knowledge, and from a general survey of things below, is very proper. But when a wish to die is merely the result of passion, a sort of quarreling with God as a child sometimes quarrels with its parents, it has more of folly in it than of wisdom and much more of petulance than of piety! It was a remarkable thing that the man who was never to die, for whom God had ordained an infinitely better lot, the man who was to be carried to Heaven by a whirlwind in a chariot of fire drawn by horses of fire—the man who, like Enoch, was "translated that he should not see death"—should thus pray to die!

We have here a memorable proof that God does not always literally answer prayer, though He always does in effect. He gave Elijah something better than that for which he asked, so He really did hear and answer his prayer. But it was strange that Elijah should have asked to die—and blessedly kind was it on the part of our Heavenly Father that He did not take His servant at his word and snatch him away at once, but spared him, that he might escape the sharpness of death.

There is, Beloved, a limit to the Doctrine of the Prayer of Faith. We are not to expect that God will give us everything for which we choose to ask. We know that we sometimes ask and do not receive because we "ask amiss" (James 4:3). If we ask contrary to the promises of God—if we run counter to the spirit which the Lord would have us cultivate—if we ask anything contrary to His will, or to the decrees of His Providence—if we ask merely for the gratification of our own ease and without an eye to His Glory, we must not expect that we shall receive. Yet, when we ask in faith, nothing doubting—if we receive not the precise thing asked for, we shall receive an equivalent and more than an equivalent for it! As one remarks, "If the Lord does not pay in silver, He will in gold. And if He does not pay in gold, He will in diamonds. If He does not give you precisely what you ask for, He will give you that which is more than tantamount to it and that which you will greatly rejoice to receive in lieu thereof."

Desiring to Die a Rational Thing
However, Elijah's faintness took this particular form of a desire to die—nor is this very uncommon, especially among the hard-worked and most eminent servants of God. This fainting fit is easily to be accounted for. It was the most rational thing in the world for Elijah to be sick at heart and to desire to die. Can you not see him standing alone upon Mount Carmel? There are the priests of Baal surrounding the altar. They wax warm with excitement. They cut themselves with knives and lancets, but all in vain. Then, with laughter and irony, the Prophet bids them cry aloud to their absent or sleeping god, Baal, and by-and-by the solemn testing-time comes. He bids them pour water on his altar and into the trench around it—and over the bullock and the

wood on which it was laid. There he stands, a lonely man believing in the invisible God—and believing that the invisible God can do what the visible Baal cannot do! He puts the whole matter to this one test, "The god that answers by fire, let him be God."

Great must have been the excitement of his flaming soul. If one could have felt his mighty heart beating just then, one might have wondered that his ribs could hold so marvelous an enigma! When "the fire of the LORD fell," (1 Kings 18:38) conceive, if you can, his holy rapture, his delirious joy! And think of him in the fury of the moment, when he cried, "Take the prophets of Baal! Let not one of them escape" (1 Kings 18:40). And think of him as he took them down to the Brook Kishon and, with his own hands, began the slaughter of the men condemned by the Mosaic Law to die because they had perverted the people of Israel from the worship of the Most High God!

And now do you see him as he goes to the top of Carmel and engages in prayer? He has conquered God once by bringing down fire from Heaven. He has overcome Baal and his prophets—and left their dead bodies, heaps upon heaps, by the brook's side. Now he goes up to conquer Heaven once more, by asking not for fire, but for water! He prays and seven times he bids his servant go and look for the answer. At last, a little cloud is discerned—the heavens begin to blacken. Elijah sends his servant to tell Ahab the king that the rain is coming. And then he girds up his loins and runs before the king's chariot as though he were as young of heart and as active of limb as ever!

With such a hard day's work, such stern mental toil, such marvelous spiritual exercises, is it a wonder that the man's reason did not reel? But instead thereof, there came on that reaction which, as long as we are mortal men, must follow strong excitement—he now feels depressed and heavy—and a woman's threat cows him who could not once have been cowed by armed hosts! He who looked to Heaven and was not afraid of all its fires, is now afraid of Jezebel because she swears that she will put him to death! It is not marvelous that it should have been so, for it is just like human nature. Peter is so bold that he cuts off the ear of Malchus and yet when a little maid comes in and accuses him of being a friend of Jesus, he denies it with oaths and curses! The boldest sometimes tremble—and it may easily be accounted for on natural principles.

God's Grace for our Fainting
Do you notice how very opportunely these fainting fits come? Elijah did not faint when God's honor was at stake at the top of the mountain. There he stands as if nothing could move him! He did not faint when it was the time to slay the priests of Baal. With quick eyes and strong limbs he dashes at them and accomplishes his mighty victory. He did not faint when it was time to pray—who faints on his knees? But he does faint when it is all over! And when it does not much matter whether he faints or not. There is no particular reason why he should not—he may well learn more of God's strength and of his own weakness. He may well be laid aside now that his work is done.

Have you never noticed, dear Friends, that God wisely times the seasons when He allows you to fall into depression of spirits? He does not touch the sinew of your thigh while you are wrestling with the angel—He makes you limp when the victory is over, but not till then! "I thank God," many a Christian may say, "that when I have been cast down and dispirited, it was at a time when it did not work such fatal mischief to me and to the cause of God as it would have done if it had occurred at another season." Is not the promise, "As your days, so shall your strength be," (Deut. 33:25) a very suggestive one? When you have a heavy day's work to do, you will have the needed strength. But when you have a day of rest, you will have no strength to waste. There shall be no vigor given to spend upon our own pride, or to sacrifice to our own glory. The battle is fought and then the strength to fight it is taken away! The victory is won and, therefore, the power to win it is removed and God's servant is made to go and lie down and sleep under a juniper tree, which was, perhaps, the best thing he could do.

And these fainting fits, to which God's children are subject, though evil in themselves, prevent greater evils. Elijah would have been something more than a man if he had not felt conceited and proud, or, at least, if there had not been in him a tendency to elation of spirit when he thought of the greatness and the splendor of the deeds he had worked. Who among us, at any rate, could have borne so much honor as God put upon him without lifting our heads to the very stars? So he is made to faint. He is constrained now to admit what I am sure he always knew and felt in his heart—that all the Glory must be given to God and not to the poor frail instrument which He was pleased to use. Graciously did God send this fainting fit to check him in what would have involved him in a far more serious fall!

Even the Mighty Need God

This depression of spirits, doubtless, taught Elijah a great lesson. It needed strong teaching to instruct him. Elijah was not a man to be taught by ordinary teachers. If he could have walked into a place where others of God's servants were ministering, I think they would all have sat down and said, "Let Elijah speak! Who among us can teach him?" The mightiest of God's servants might be silent before him and, therefore, God Himself teaches him.

Some servants of the Lord are taught by God in a way which is quite unknown to others. There is a path which the eagle's eyes have not seen and which the lion's whelp has not traveled—a path of secret chastisement as well as of secret Revelation. Those whom God honors in public, He often chastens in private. Those men who shine most as candles of the Lord's own right-hand lighting are sometimes made to feel that they would be, but a snuff if the Grace of God should depart from them. God has ways of teaching all of us in our bones and in our flesh, but He specially knows how to do this with those upon whom He puts any honor in His service. You must not marvel if God should be pleased to bless you to the conversion of souls, that He should also make you sometimes smart. Remember that Paul, with all his Grace, could not be without "a thorn in the flesh." There must also be "a messenger of Satan to buffet you," lest you should be exalted above measure (2 Cor. 12:7-8)! So may you learn to submit cheerfully to a discipline which, though painful to you, your Heavenly Father knows to be wise!

Moreover, these fainting fits to which God's servants are subject, are not only profitable to those who have them, but to others. To compare small things with great, a foolish idea sometimes gets into the minds of our hearer that surely the minister can never be much cast down. Young converts sometimes think that old saints can never know such contentions within, such doubting, such humbling of spirit as they feel. Ah, but whether they are dwarfs or giants, the experience of Christian men is amazingly alike! There are lines of weakness in the creature which even Divine Grace does not efface.

"When the peacock looks at his fair feathers," says old Master Dyer, "he may afterwards look at his black feet." And so, whenever the brightest Christian begins to be proud of his graces, there will be sure to be something about him which will remind others as well as himself that he is yet in the body! I forget how many times it is that Ezekiel is called, in the book of his prophecy, "the son of man." I counted them the other day and I do not find the same title applied to any other Prophet so often as it is to him. Why is this? Why, there was never another Prophet who had such eagle wings as Ezekiel had! It was given to him to soar more loftily than any other! And therefore he is always called, "the son of man," to show that he is but a man after all.

Your highest people, your most elevated saints are but sons of fallen Adam, touched with the same infirmities and weaknesses as their fellow creatures and liable, unless Grace prevents, to fall into the same sins as others fall into! I think these are good and sufficient reasons why the strongest Believers often experience the most oppressive weakness.

Refreshment from God for our Fainting
Now let us turn to a second thought, which is this— When believers do have fainting fits, they will receive extraordinary refreshments.

Elijah had often been fed in a remarkable manner. Ravens had ministered to his necessities at one time and at another time an impoverished widow had boarded him. But on this occasion he is to be fed by an angel. The best refreshments are to be provided for him at the worst season! He might well have said, "You have kept the best wine until now, when I needed it the most." The food that he ate at Cherith had to be brought to him every morning and every evening, but the food which was now given to him lasted him for forty days and forty nights—and though the widow's cruse did not fail, yet he needed to apply to it constantly. But in this case, one meal, or rather a double meal, was sufficient to last him during six weeks of journeying! He was supernaturally awakened. He found food convenient for him—a cake and a cruse of water all ready at his hand—he had only to rise and take it!

Now, my dear Brothers and Sisters in Christ—for I now speak only to you—have you never found that in times when heart and flesh have both failed, you have been privileged to receive some special help from Heaven? Sometimes it has come to you in the form of a full assurance of your interest in Christ. Your heart was very heavy. The work you had before you seemed to be much too arduous for you. Your spirit quailed before your enemies. The weight of your trouble was too much for you, but just then Jesus whispered softly into your ear that you were His! You had doubted before whether you really were Christ's, but you could not doubt it any longer—the Spirit bore witness with your spirit that you were born of God and you could—

"Read your title clear, to mansions in the skies!"[2]

It is amazing how this assurance acts in two ways. It is the great cure for us when we are soaring too high. When Christ's disciples had cast out devils, He said to them, "Notwithstanding in this rejoice not, that the spirits are subject unto you, but rather rejoice because your names are written in Heaven" (Luke 10:20). And this, too, is the cure for us when we fall too low. Mourn not over this, but still "rejoice because your names are written in Heaven." Many an old saint, sitting in a chimney corner under an accumulation of aches, pains, weaknesses and sorrows, has sung—

> When I can read my title clear
> To mansions in the skies,
> I bid farewell to every fear,
> And wipe my weeping eyes.
> Should earth against my soul engage,
> And hellish darts be hurled,
> Then I can smile at Satan's rage,
> And face a frowning world.[3]

Bless God for the full assurance of faith, for it will yield you food in the strength of which you may go on for forty days and forty nights. May God give us to feed on it constantly! But sometimes He gives us the richest meal of it just when we are in our weakest state and are ready to give up in despair.

We have known the Lord feed His people, sometimes, with another Truth of God, namely, the Doctrine of His

---

2. Isaac Watts.

3. ibid.

own greatness and grandeur. A sight of the greatness of God is a very blessed stay to us under a sense of our littleness. There you lie, broken and bruised, like an insect that has been crushed. You look up and the light flashes through the dark cloud and you behold something of the greatness and the Glory of God and you think, "What are my troubles? He can bear them! What are all my griefs? They are only as the small dust of the balance to Him. Why should I faint or grow weary when He upon whom I lean faints not, neither is weary? Underneath me are His everlasting arms. He is mighty, though I am a thing of naught. He is wise, though I am lost, bewildered and foolish. He is faithful, though I am doubting and trembling. "The more His glories strike our eyes"[4]—the less apt shall we be to die of despair! We shall feed upon this food as Elijah did upon his cake baked upon the coals and, like he, we shall go in the strength of it for forty days!

Sometimes, too, we have known the blessedness of feeding upon the assurance that the cause of God will be ultimately triumphant. I remember when, like a broken, bruised and worthless thing, I seemed set aside from Christian service and from my work for God which I loved. It seemed to me as though I should never return again to preach the Word. I marveled how the work of my hands under God would fare and my spirit was overwhelmed within me. I made diligent search after comfort, but found none. My soul took counsel within herself and so increased her woes, but no light came. I shall never forget the moment when, all of a sudden, these words came to me.

---

4. Isaac Watts, "659" in *An Arrangement of the Psalms, Hymns and Spiritual Songs of Isaac Watts* https://books.google.com/books (accessed April 1, 2015).

> Therefore God also has highly exalted Him and given Him a name which is above every name; that at the name of Jesus every knee should bow, of things in Heaven, and things in earth, and things under the earth; and that every tongue should confess that Jesus Christ is Lord, to the glory of God the Father (Phil. 2:9-11).

At once I thought, "What matters if I, the soldier, fall upon the battlefield, if my great Captain is safe? Jehovah reigns! Christ is exalted!" Then I seemed to look upon my own being set aside—my shame, my reproach, my death, or anything else that might befall me—as not being worth a moment's thought because the King stood yonder and the blood-red flag waved in triumph! O God, Your Truth must conquer in the end! Your foes must flee! What if they gain some petty advantage here and there along the line? What if they do make a breach here and there in the bulwarks of our Zion? They shall fly like chaff before the wind in the day when You appear! The battle is Yours, O Lord, and You will deliver them into our hands before long!

Let the ultimate triumph of the Truth of God solace you when you are discouraged because you have seemed to labor in vain and spent your strength for naught. Be of good cheer—the Conqueror who comes with dyed garments from Bozrah, is still in the midst of His Church! This cake baked on the coals has often given food to poor fainting Elijahs.

The Sympathy of Jesus

A conviction, too, of the sympathy of Jesus Christ with them has often been very dainty food and a precious cordial to mourning spirits. This is, perhaps, the very first Doctrine we teach the bereaved and sick saints. We tell them that "in all their afflictions He was afflicted" (Isa. 63:9). And probably there is no verse that is sung more often and with greater sweetness than this one—

> How bitter that cup no heart can conceive,
> Which He drank quite up, that sinners might live!
> His way was much rougher and darker than mine—
> Did Jesus thus suffer, and shall I repine?[5]

It makes pain so glorious when you think that the very same pain shoots through Him as through you, that there is not so much pain truly in the finger as there is in the head, that the head is indeed the true seat of all the sensitiveness. It is not so much Christ's people who suffer, as it is Christ, Himself, suffering in them. Does it not make the Cross glorious when you bear it with the thought that it is Christ's Cross you are carrying? To suffer poverty for Christ's sake is a very different thing from suffering poverty in the abstract. To be despised for the Gospel's sake is a different thing from being despised for any other reason for, to be reproached for Christ is honor—and to suffer for Christ is pleasure!

A mother will sit up night after night to nurse her darling child. She would not do it for anyone else for any money you could offer her—and though she grows very weary, she goes to her work and does for her child what she would not and probably could not do for any other child. So some of us would do for love what we would not think of doing for gain. And when we know that we are doing and suffering for Christ—and feel that Christ is with us in

---

5. John Newton, "Begone Unbelief" http://www.hymntime.com/tch/htm/b/e/g/begonunb.htm (accessed April 2, 2015)

it all, it becomes a very blessed cordial and we—"Rejoice in deep distress"[6]—since Jesus Christ is with us!

Contemplating Heaven

And how often has God given much comfort to His people when they were ready to give all up, by a vision of Heaven? Did you ever have such a vision? Softly will it sometimes steal over your spirit, especially in severe sickness, when heaviness and uneasiness seem to bring you to the very gates of the grave. You do not hear the bells of Heaven with your ears, nor do stray notes of angels' harps salute you, nor do you see the white-robed hosts with your natural eyes, but your soul sees and hears it all! God sometimes brings His people into "the land of Beulah" before they fairly reach it in the order in which John Bunyan puts it in his allegory.

Some of us have been to the very gates of Heaven. We have had such foretastes of Heaven that we feel that we can now fight the fight and cheerfully wait—"Our threescore years and ten" (Ps. 90:10)—if the Lord pleases to spare us so long, because the crown at the end is so glorious! And that we can journey through the wilderness because the Canaan is so worthy of all that we can do or suffer that we may enter it.

Beloved, a vision of Jesus Christ and a vision of Heaven will be enough to solace the most downcast among you! And where you gladly would hang your harp upon the willows, if Jesus Christ shall appear to you and His Father shall smile upon you, and His Spirit shall actively work upon your hearts, and Heaven's gate shall be opened to

---

6. Isaac Watts, "Hymn 15" in *Psalms and Hymns of Isaac Watts* http://www.ccel.org/ccel/watts/psalmshymns.I.15.html (accessed April 2, 2015).

you—then will you snatch up your harp and wake it to the sweetest melodies in praise of Sovereign Grace! You Elijahs who are now saying, "Let me die," change your note, for there is a cake baked on the coals provided for you—so arise and eat it!

Strength and Solitude

Let us observe, in the third place, that whenever God thus gives to his children very remarkable enjoyments, it is in order that they may go on in the strength of those enjoyments for a long time.

Elijah was not fed that he might get strong and then waste his strength. There are no sinecures in God's service! All His true servants are real workmen and when they have strength given to them by Him, it is not that they may show what fine fellows they are, but that they may toil on in their Master's cause. The soldier is a smart-looking fellow on parade in days of peace—and long may it be before he shall have cause to do anything more than show himself at such times—but God's soldiers are always on active service and as sure as ever the Master gives them a double round of ammunition, He means them to fire it all! If ever He gives them a new sword, it is because they will soon need it! And whenever He is pleased to furnish them with fresh armor, it is because He knows that they will require the sacred panoply. There are no superfluities in the provisions of God's Grace!

[margin note: A position that require No work]

What had Elijah to do? Having fed upon this angels' food, he had to go a long solitary journey. I wonder whether you can imagine it—a journey of forty days and forty nights! It does not seem to me, from what I gather from the story, that he ever stopped. Certainly he did not stop to take refreshments, but went right away into the

63

wilderness, having probably left his servant at Beersheba the whole time. He never saw the face of man all the while. He fasted more wonderfully than Moses did, who fasted on the mountain in peace and quietness! This mysterious Prophet fasted and at the same time he was taking giant strides in the lonely wilderness, startling the beasts of prey, treading the unfrequented tracts of the wild goats and the gazelles with ever-onward feet! On through the day's burning heat and the night's black shade, never pausing for forty days and forty nights! A strange march was that, but sometimes God calls His people to something very much like it.

Strange, weird-like and solitary is your soul—and nobody can walk with you where you have to go—you have to take strides that will suit no one else. You have to go a way that has not been trodden before by any others. The Master has called you to special suffering, if not to special service. You have no pioneer and no companion. I suppose every person who is called to serve God in a remarkable manner, or to suffer for Him in a particular way, must have noticed the solitariness of his own life.

Do not tell me about solitude being only in the wilderness—a man may have plenty of company there— the worst solitude is that which a man may have among millions of his fellow creatures. Look at that solitude of Moses. When Moses had his heaviest cares upon him, with whom could he hold any real communion? With the seventy elders? As well might an eagle have stooped to have communion with so many sparrows! They were far beneath him—they had not hearts large enough to commune with the great-souled Moses. You will say, perhaps, that Aaron might have done so. Yes, truly, a brother's heart is a very cheering one when it beats to the same tune as your own, but Aaron was a man of altogether different spirit from Moses and nobody would think of comparing the two men! Moses is like some of those colossal figures that are cut in the Egyptian rocks, or that stand amidst the ruins of Karnak—he seems to have been one of those great spirits of the grand olden time before the stature of men had declined—and he is all alone. He bears the people on his bosom and throughout his life is a solitary man.

Such, too, was Elijah. Now, perhaps you will have special feasting upon Christ because in your trial or in your labor you will have to learn that there is a secret you cannot tell to any but your God—that there is a bitterness with which no other heart can intermeddle—that there are heights and depths through which you will have to pass and will have to pass alone. Do not wonder, dear Friends, if these words should come true to you in days to come. Do not marvel if that verse we sometimes sing should happen to be suitable to you on this quiet, peaceful evening—"We should suspect some danger near, when we perceive too much delight." If God feeds us with angels' food, He means us to do more than man's work.

The Purposes of our Long Journey

But I meant you to notice, in the next place, that while Elijah was thus fed that he might go a long and lonely journey, that he was sent on that journey that he might be brought into more sympathy with God than before. Why did he have to journey "forty days and forty nights into Horeb the mount of God"? It is said that it was not more than eighty miles and certainly does not appear to have been 100. Such a long time was not necessary for the distance—why, therefore, did Elijah take it? Do you not see that it is a day for a year? "Forty years long," says Jehovah, "was I grieved with this generation" in the wilderness. Forty days and nights, therefore, must the Lord's servant walk over the very tracks where Israel had pitched their tents. And God seemed to say to him, "O Elijah, do you lose your temper and turn away from Israel, and ask to die, when I had to bear with My people forty years and yet, notwithstanding that, they now inherit the goodly land and have come to Lebanon?"

Beloved, the servants of God must frequently meet with ingratitude, unkind treatment, harsh words and cruel speeches from those whom they try to serve! And sometimes God's own people are a greater plague to God's ministers than are all the rest of the world besides. Well, what of that? Does not the Lord seem to say, "Now I will teach you what My compassions are. I will teach you what My patience must be. You shall have forty days' walking in the wilderness to make you understand something of what I felt when, for forty years, I bore with the ill manners, rebellions and idolatries of this crooked and perverse people"? Is it not a grand thing, my Brothers and Sisters, to be made to have sympathy with God? I do not think the most of Christians understand this— to be made to feel as God felt so that you are enabled, as it were, to see things from God's standpoint and to begin to understand why He is angry with the wicked—and to magnify that matchless Grace which bears so long with the sons of men!

It may possibly happen, that the Master has been feeding you upon some special and dainty food at His table, or under the ministry, or in earnest prayer, or in communion, or in meditation in order that, in the future, you may have greater sympathy with Himself by treading, in your measure, the same path that He trod in years long gone by!

There is always a special reason when there comes a special mercy, and so, to conclude, I ask you to note that the Lord gave His servant this special benefit because He intended to give him a very special rebuke.

Gracious Words: Harder and Softer

"What are you doing here, Elijah?" was not the sort of language that Elijah had been accustomed to hear from his God! He could use such language, himself, to his fellow men, as he did when he spoke to Ahab, but he was not accustomed to hear such words spoken to him by God! Softer sentences had greeted his ears, but now God is about to rebuke him for running away from his work, for playing the coward and for setting an example of unbelief!

But before He rebukes him, He supplies all his needs and gives him forty days' strength. The Lord does not chasten His children when they are weak and sickly, "without," as one says, "sustaining them with one hand while He smites them with the other." He will give you comforting grace as well as the privilege of chastisement. You cannot do without the rod, but you shall be enabled, on the strength of the food which He will give you, to bear up under it without your spirit utterly fainting.

Possibly God may have in store for some of us a special rebuke. He may intend to make some thundering passage in His Word come with terrific power to our souls. He may mean to lay us upon a bed of sickness and, therefore, now, by giving us strengthening food, He is preparing us for it, that even when in the furnace we may be enabled to sing His praise!

I leave these thoughts with those of you who know the way of the wilderness. Those of you who do not will not care much about them, but I may pray God that the sinner who knows nothing of these faintings, may be made to faint utterly till his soul dies within him with spiritual despair! And when he so dies, then the Lord who kills will make him alive! When you have no power left, if you can throw yourself beneath the shadow of the Cross, though your flesh may make you sleep there as Elijah did under the juniper tree, yet you shall hear a voice which shall bid you arise—and in the great Atonement of the Savior you shall find a cake baked on what hot coals I will not now undertake to say. You shall find it such food to the weary spirit that when you have partaken of it, poor Sinner, you shall dare to go to the mount of God, even to Horeb, and face the terrible Law of God and ask, "Who shall lay anything to my charge?"

Feeding on Jesus, mysteriously sustained by trusting in the efficacy of His precious blood, you shall go on till you shall see God face to face in His holy mount in Glory, in the strength of Him who said, "For My flesh is meat indeed, and My blood is drink indeed."

God bless every one of us, for Jesus' sake! Amen.

4

Elijah Fainting[1]

*"He himself went a day's journey into the
wilderness, and came and sat down under a
juniper tree: and he requested for himself that he
might die; and said, It is enough; now, O LORD,
take away my life; for I am no better
than my fathers."*
(1 Kings 19:4)

When we read the Scriptures in our youth, we are often astonished at the peculiar conditions in which we find even good men. It is difficult for us to understand why David could be in such sore distress and why such a man as Elijah could be so dreadfully downcast. As we get older and become more experienced, as trials multiply around us and our inner life enters upon a sterner conflict—as

---

1. Charles Spurgeon, "Elijah Fainting," *Metropolitan Tabernacle Pulpit*, Vol. 47, No. 2725 www.spurgeongems.org (accessed March 9, 2015).

the babe grows to manhood and, therefore, is entrusted with heavier tasks, we can better understand why God allowed His ancient servants to be put into such peculiar positions, for we find ourselves in similar places—and we are relieved by discovering that we are walking along a path which others have traversed before us.

It might puzzle us to tell why Elijah should get under a juniper bush. We can understand his attitude on Mount Carmel and comprehend his hewing the Prophets of Baal in pieces, but we ask, in perplexity, "What are you doing here, Elijah, under a juniper, or away there in a cave on the hillside?" But when we get under the juniper, ourselves, we are glad to recall the fact that Elijah once sat there—and when we are hiding away in the cave, it is a source of comfort to us to remember that such a man as this great Prophet of Israel was there before us. The experience of one saint is instructive to others. Many of those Psalms which are headed, "Maschil," or instructive Psalms, record the experience of the writer and, therefore, become the lesson book for others.

I may be, at this time, addressing some of the Lord's children who have prayed Elijah's prayer. I know one who, in the bitterness of his soul, has often prayed it and, if God the Comforter shall guide me, I may be able to say something that shall help such an one in this, his time of trial. If I should be permitted to come as God's angel to smite some sleeper on the side and wake him up to eat of spiritual meat which shall cause him to forget his sorrow, it shall be well. I will, first, speak about Elijah's weakness. And then, in the second place, about God's tenderness to him.

Even our Strongest are Still Human

First, I am going to speak about Elijah's weakness. Only a few days before, he had stood on Mount Carmel as the mighty Prophet of God and had brought down from Heaven first fire and then water—he seemed to have the very keys of the skies and to be girt almost with Omnipotence to do whatever he would when he lifted up his voice in prayer! Yet, soon after, he was fleeing from the face of Jezebel, lest she should take him and put him to death! And here we find him, after a long flight in the wilderness, sitting down under a juniper bush, seeking to find a scanty shelter there—and entreating that he may die. Why?

Well, the first reason is, that he was a man of like passions with ourselves. I suppose that the Apostle James would hardly have said that concerning him if he had not perceived its truth in this particular instance (James 5:17). We used to have, in England, a great leader who is still called, "The Iron Duke." I think we might have called Elijah, "The Iron Prophet." He seemed to leap into the field of action like a lion from the forest. What strength and courage he had! He seemed to have nothing of the timidity, trembling and weakness of ordinary manhood—he was a very athlete in the service of God, girding up his loins and running before Ahab's chariot.

Yet here we see that he was, indeed, a man of like passions with ourselves. He, too, could be impatient. He, too, could be petulant. He, too, could grow weary of his appointed service and ask to be allowed to die. You have often heard me say that the best of men are but men at the best.

The other day somebody wrote me a letter to tell me that sentence was not true. All I could reply was, "No doubt, my good Friend, you know yourself and if, at your best, you are not a man, I do not know what you are—you must be something worse." And there I left him.

But I believe that when a man is as good as he can be, he is still only a man—and as a man, while he is here, he is compassed with infirmities. Elijah was not only a man of passions, but a man of like passions with ourselves—a man who could suffer, and suffer intensely. He was one whose spirit could be depressed even to the very uttermost, just as the spirit of any one of us might be. He failed, as all God's people have done! I scarcely know of any exception in all the biographies of the Old or New Testament.

Elijah failed in the very point at which he was strongest, and that is where most men fail. In Scripture, it is the wisest man who proves himself to be the greatest fool. Just as the meekest man, Moses, spoke hasty and bitter words. Abraham failed in his faith and Job in his patience. So, he who was the most courageous of all men fled from an angry woman! He could stand face to face with that woman's husband and say to him, in answer to his false accusation, "I have not troubled Israel; but you, and your father's house, in that you have forsaken the commandments of the LORD, and you have followed Baalim" (1 Kings 18:18). Yet he was afraid of Jezebel and he fled from her—and suffered such faintness of heart that he even "requested for himself that he might die."

This was, I suppose, to show us that Elijah was not strong by nature, but only in the strength imparted to him by God, so that, when the Divine strength was gone, he was of no more account than anybody else. When Grace is for a time withdrawn, the natural Elijah is as weak as any other natural man! It is only when supernatural power is working through him that he rises out of himself—and so the Grace of God is glorified in him.

It is some comfort to us when we see that we are not the only persons who have failed through the infirmity of the flesh. I do not hold up Elijah's passions as any excuse for us indulging them, but if any are almost driven to despair because such passions have overcome them, let them shake off that despair. Nobody doubts that Elijah was a child of God! Nobody questions the fact that God loved him even when he sat fainting under the juniper tree, for He manifested special love to him then—so let no despondent heart, no broken spirit, no discouraged soul say—

"My God has quite forsaken me,
My God will be gracious no more"[2]

— for it is not true! The Lord did not forsake Elijah and He will not forsake you if you trust in Him.

Soaring and Descending

Yet it may be that both you and Elijah have cherished passions of which He does not approve. But, next, let us notice that this faintness of heart of Elijah was, no doubt, the result of a terrible reaction which had come upon his whole frame. On that memorable day when all Israel was gathered together, and he stood forth as a lone man to champion the cause of Jehovah, having the 450 Prophets of Baal and the 400 Prophets of the groves in opposition to him, there must have been a strong excitement upon him.

2.　Augustus Toplady, "Encompass'd with Clouds of Distress."
http://www.hymnary.org/text/encompassed_with_clouds_of_distress
(accessed April 4, 2015)

You can see that he was not very calm when the two altars stood side by side and the prophets of Baal from morning till noon cried in vain, "O Baal, hear us." Somehow, I like to think of Elijah in the splendid furor of his soul, mocking them, and saying, "Cry aloud, for he is a god! Either he is talking, or he is pursuing, or he is on a journey, or perhaps he sleeps and must be awaked!" And, in their fanaticism, they cried aloud and cut themselves after their manner with knives and lancets.

Elijah's blood was up to fever heat, his whole soul was aroused and he scoffed at and scorned those who could worship anything except the one true God! And what a time of excitement that must have been when he bade the people go and fetch water from the sea and pour it on the bullock and the wood lying upon Jehovah's altar. When they had done as he bade them, he said, "Do it the second time." And then, "Do it the third time." And then, when the water ran round about the altar and filled the trench as well, he prayed, and said, "LORD God of Abraham, Isaac, and of Israel, let it be known this day that You are God in Israel, and that I am Your servant, and that I have done all these things at Your word. Hear me, O LORD, hear me, that this people may know that You are the LORD God, and that You have turned their heart back again. Then the fire of the LORD fell and consumed the burnt sacrifice, and the wood, and the stones, and the dust, and licked up the water that was in the trench. And when all the people saw it, they fell on their faces and said, "The LORD, He is the God; the LORD, He is the God' (1 Kings 18:20-39).

I suppose that Elijah had no trembling while the issue of the conflict was in suspense. I expect that he felt the utmost assurance that the fire would come down—but even that confidence must have been accompanied by a wonderful excitement of spirit while he stood gazing up into Heaven and crying to God to send the fire as His answering signal from the sky. I can imagine, too, the intense delight and the holy triumph of the Prophet when it came! And I can conceive how the grand Prophetic frenzy came upon him, making him to become both judge and executioner as he exclaimed, "Take the Prophets of Baal; let not one of them escape."

Then, when he had executed the stern vengeance of God upon them, he had to go up to the top of Carmel and pray for the rain. That was another season of intense strain upon his mind. And when he had sent to Ahab the message, "Prepare your chariot, and get you down, that the rain stop you not," the old Prophet did what must have been very unusual for a man of his age and position, for he girded up his loins, and ran, like a footman, before the king, to prove his loyalty! So I do not wonder that when the day's work was done, he was very weary. And when the news came that Jezebel had determined to put him to death, his heart sank within him. As he had risen high, so he fell low. As he had soared, he must descend.

It seems to be the way with us all—we must pay the price for any joy that we experience. We cannot have great exhilaration without having some measure of depression afterwards. Do not condemn yourself if this is your lot. Do not excuse yourself if there is any measure of unbelief mingled with your depression, but do not condemn yourself for what is really as natural a result as the retirement of the sea after its waves have kissed the cliff.

It must be so—night must follow day, winter must succeed to summer—and joyful spirits that rise aloft must sink again. We may sometimes wish that we could always keep on the level ground where some of our dear friends live. I have often envied them, especially when I have been down in the dumps. But when I have again ascended to the heights, I have not envied them in the least. At such times I would have pulled them up with me if it had been possible! But that I could not do. So, dear friend, you may depend upon it that you cannot be Elijah upon Carmel without the probability that you will be Elijah under a juniper bush before long. The great Prophet of fire proves himself to be only a man, after all—and in the time of testing you, also, will be as weak as other men.

Depression from Spiritual Disappointment

Another reason for the Prophet's depression was, no doubt, his intense love to God and his grievous disappointment with the people. He had hoped that the test he had proposed would decide the great question, "If Jehovah is God, follow Him: but if Baal, then follow him." He had staked everything upon that one issue, "The God that answers by fire, let Him be God." And he had proved to a demonstration that Jehovah was God. Israel ought to have renewed her covenant and to have returned to the God of her fathers then and there, but that wicked woman Jezebel had power over the people and as long as she ruled the court, and the court ruled the nation, the cause of God could not come to the front. Elijah could not endure that and I think that the heaviest sorrows to a really gracious heart are the sins of the times, the transgressions of the multitude, the national sins that bite like asps into an earnest soul, especially if you have done something, or have seen it done by others which ought to have ended the discussion and settled the matter once and for all.

Sometimes, when we have trusted in God and He has worked a great deliverance, and when this has been done before the eyes of men who, if it had not been worked would have denied God's existence or power, we have been disappointed to find that they did not candidly go the other way and say, "Since God has done this, we are bound to admit that there is power in prayer, and that God's promises in the Scriptures are not a dead letter." No, my Brothers and Sisters, they would not be convinced even though God should rend the azure sky and put out His own right hand visibly before them! They would still say, "There is no God," and they would talk of the phenomenon which they had seen and, no doubt, interpret it upon some natural or scientific principles so as to fritter the whole thing away!

This kind of conduct eats into a godly man's spirit and there is not much cause to wonder that he who could say, "I have been very jealous for the Lord God of Hosts," should find himself in such a state of heart that he steals right away into the wilderness and never wants to see anybody again. Have you never sighed, as did the poet Cowper—

"O for a lodge in some vast wilderness,
Some boundless contiguity of shade,
Where rumor of oppression and deceit
Of unsuccessful or successful war
Might never reach me more"[3]

—or have you never used the language of David, "Oh that I had wings like a dove! For then would I fly away, and be at rest" (Ps. 55:6)?

---

3. William Cowper, "Book Two: The Time Piece," in *The Task*. http://www.ccel.org/c/cowper/works/task.htm (accessed April 7, 2015).

Weariness and Anxieties

There was, probably, another and a minor reason for Elijah's great depression, that is, he was very weary. I should suppose that he had gone a very long way without resting at all. Hot foot in hasty flight from the cruel Jezebel, he had passed through a great part of the land both of Israel and Judah and he had gone away alone into the wilderness. So he must have been very tired and that, of itself, would tend to the lowering of his spirits. It is always a pity, when you are taking stock of yourself, not to consider the condition of the weather, the state of your stomach and liver, and a great many other things. Though they may seem small, yet there may be more in them than is apparent to the sight.

I have known a man feel so bad that he thought he could not be a child of God, when, really, the main trouble was that he needed his dinner—for his spirits revived as soon as he had partaken of proper nourishment. Certainly, one of the lessons that this chapter teaches us is that when we get weary, or we suffer from some disease, so that the strength of our body begins to flag, then we are apt to say—

"Tis a point I long to know,
Oft it causes anxious thought—
Do I love the Lord, or no?
Am I His, or am I not?"[4]

Now that kind of anxiety is right enough, but sometimes the cause of it lies in some small thing, altogether apart from spiritual forces, yet something which the devil can use to torment us very much. You know how Paul was

---

4.   John Newton, *Olney Hymns* (London: W. Oliver, 1779), number 119.
     http://www.hymntime.com/tch/htm/t/i/s/tispoint.htm
     (accessed April 7, 2015).

tormented by Satan, once, in a way that was very painful and trying. It was not the devil himself who came to him—it was "the messenger of Satan"—one of his errand boys. And he did not come to wound the Apostle with a sword—he only came to "buffet" him, to hit him, as it were, with a gloved hand. And when he pierced him, it was only with "a thorn in the flesh" (2 Cor. 12:1-7).

Yet that little thing bothered the Apostle so much that he could not endure it and he had to cry to God about it. He says, "For this thing I besought the Lord thrice, that it might depart from me." It often happens that some little thing like that, which really, at another time, we should altogether despise, may be the cause of intense depression of spirit. I know it is so and I beseech God's children, however unusual the advice may seem, to attach some importance to it, or else they may begin condemning themselves when there is nothing to condemn and accusing themselves when they are really right with God and all things are prospering with them.

What terrible pain you may suffer from a little speck of dust in one of your eyes! You cannot see it, but you can feel it—and the tiniest stone in your shoe—how difficult it makes your walking! And other little things will, often, as in the case of the Prophet's weariness, cause grievous depression of spirit.

Follies Hidden in our Desire to Die

I must, however, point out to you that Elijah's prayer that he might die was a very foolish one. Let us look at it a minute or two, and its folly will soon appear. He prayed that he might die. Why? Because he was afraid that he would die! That is the odd thing about his request—he was running away from Jezebel because she had threatened to kill him, yet he prayed that he might die! This was very inconsistent on his part, but we always are inconsistent when we are unbelieving. There is nothing in the world more ridiculous than unbelieving fears. If we could but see them as we shall see them one day, when faith is strong and we get into clearer light, we would laugh at ourselves and then weep over ourselves to think that we should be so foolish. You run away from death and then ask that you may die—that is what Elijah did, so it is no cause for wonder if poor ordinary mortals, such as we are, act in the same fashion as this great Prophet of God did!

Further, it was great folly for him to wish to die because there was more need, even according to his own account, that he should continue to live then than there ever had been before. What did he say? "I, even I only, am left; and they seek my life, to take it away." But, Elijah, if you die, there will be an end of the Lord's people if your reckoning is correct! Surely, if you are the only one left, you ought to pray that you may live on until there are some more to carry on the work. It is a pity that the coal of Israel should be utterly quenched and that the last lamp should be put out. The reason that the Prophet gave for wanting to die was the very best reason he could have given for wanting to live!

That is strange, but we are very strange creatures. There is not a man here who is not foolish at times—certainly, he who is in the pulpit takes precedence over you all in that respect—we all, some time or other, let out the folly that is in us, and we only need to be driven up into a corner, as Elijah was, and our folly will be discovered as was his! He ought to have prayed to live, yet he prayed that he might die!

Another thing that proves his folly is that he never was to die at all, and he never did die, for he went up by a whirlwind into Heaven! It is a remarkable fact that he who prayed that he might die is one of the two men who leaped over the ditch of death and entered into life without dying! I wonder whether, as he rode to Heaven in that chariot of fire, Elijah said to himself, "Why, I am the man who prayed that I might die!" If he did, he must have smiled with holy wonder that God did not take him at his word—and with sacred pleasure that his prayer was left unanswered. It was a petition that never ought to have been presented and you and I, Beloved, often have good reason to thank God that He does not answer our prayers. We may sing with quaint Ralph Erskine—

"I'm heard when answered soon or late
And heard when I no answer get.
Yes, kindly answered when refused,
And friendly treated when harshly used."[5]

So was it with the Prophet Elijah—God answered him by not answering him because He had in store for him some better thing than he had asked!

Note, also, that the reason Elijah gave for his prayer was an untrue one. He said, "It is enough; now, O Lord, take away my life." But it was not enough—he had not done enough for his Lord. He thought that he had. He imagined that he had gone to the very verge of his capacity. He had exalted God in the midst of the people and put the whole nation to a crucial test, so he said, "It is enough. I can do

---

5. Ralph Erskine, *Gospel Sonnets; Or, Spiritual Songs* (Edinburgh: W. Darling, 1782), 170. https://books.google.com/books (accessed April 7, 2015).

no more." But he had a great deal more to do! He had to go down to Naboth's vineyard and charge Ahab with the guilt of Naboth's death. He had to rebuke the idolatry of Ahaziah and, above all, he had to call out his successor, who would keep the Prophetic lamp burning in the midst of Israel! Elijah said, "It is enough," yet it was not enough even for his own enjoyment, for the Lord had more blessings in store for him!

And you and I, Beloved, have often felt that we have been, like Naphtali, "satisfied with favour, and full with the blessing of the LORD" (Deut. 33:23), yet the Lord has given us still richer favors and choicer blessings. It was so with Elijah, for he was to have that wonderful revelation of God on Mount Horeb. He had more to enjoy and the later life of Elijah appears to have been one of calm communion with his God. He seems never to have had another fainting fit, but to the end his sun shone brightly without a cloud. So it was not enough!

But how could he know that it was? It is God alone who knows when we have done enough and enjoyed enough— we do not know. Elijah also said, "O Lord, take away my life; for I am no better than my fathers." But that was probably no more true than was the other reason that he gave for wishing to die. We do not know anything about his father, or any of his ancestors, but it is not likely that any one of them was at all comparable to him. Elijah was a grand man, a truly great man! God had favored him far beyond his fathers and intended to still do so. He was a man who walked altogether on a higher path than the rest of his fellows and while it was well for him to be humble, it was not well for him to be so humble as to forget the great things that God had done for him.

Come, then, my dear Brother or Sister, if you are sitting under your juniper tree and saying, "Let me die, for it is enough." Correct your foolish request—examine the reason that suggests it and you will find it too weak to justify such a desire! And so may God help you to abandon it at once!

The Tenderness of God in our Prayers to Die

Now, in the second place, it is a very pleasing task to speak for a few minutes upon God's tenderness to Elijah in this time of weakness. It is always well for ministers, and all who have the care of souls, to watch how God deals with those who are in trouble, just as a young surgeon, when he walks the hospital, is eager to see how a master in the healing art treats his patients.

The first thing that God did with Elijah was a very simple thing, he let him sleep. There is the poor Prophet down in the dumps—he wants to die but the Lord lets him sleep, instead—and he slept soundly, too, for he needed an angel to wake him! And soon he fell asleep again and a second time he had to be awakened. Rest was the one thing that he most needed, so, by—"Tired nature's sweet restorer, balmy sleep"[6]—God gave His servant rest. Some people do not seem to think that the Lord's servants need any rest. They want us to be always at work, fulfilling this engagement and that. But this is the way to bring us quickly to our graves! Yet we do not serve a hard Master— His Church is often thoughtless and unkind, but He never is, so He gave His servant Elijah the sleep that he most of all needed just then.

---

6.   Edward Young, *Night Thoughts*, Line 1 (London: 1743)
http://www.gutenberg.org/files/33156/33156-h/33156-h.htm
(accessed April 7, 2015).

What was the next thing that God did? It seems a very small matter, yet it was the best thing he could do for Elijah. That is, the Lord fed him. When the angel awakened him, "he looked, and, behold, there was a cake baked on the coals, and a cruse of water at his head. And he did eat and drink and laid him down again" (1 Kings 19:6).

Now, I am afraid that if you and I had been there, we should have begun talking to Elijah and have worried the poor man by telling him how wrongly he had been acting. Instead of doing that, the angel let him have a cake and then let him go back to sleep. That was the best way of caring for him—and there is many a hungry and weary child of God who needs food and rest more than anything else. The spirit needs to be fed and the body needs feeding also. Do not forget these matters! It may seem to some people that I ought not to mention such small things as food and rest, but these may be the very first elements in really helping a poor depressed servant of God. It is not surprising that God becomes Cake-Maker to His children, for we know that He is their Bed-Maker.

David said, concerning the man who considers the poor, "The Lord will strengthen him upon the bed of languishing: You will make all his bed in his sickness" (Ps. 41:3). There is nothing that is really necessary or beneficial which God will not do for His children. If they serve Him so zealously that they get banged up in His service, he will care for them and bring them round again, for He knows how to do it. And very likely, like Elijah, they shall have their sleep, first, and then their cake.

The next comfort that Elijah had was blessed nursing. He had an angelic visitor to keep him company. The angel came to him and delivered the Lord's message, "Arise: eat."

He only uttered two words, but two words from an angel are better than a great many from some other persons! "Arise: eat." That was God's message to Elijah and, Beloved, it is very sweet when God lets His servants know that His angels are round about them, encompassing them, taking care of them, as when Jacob was met at Mahanaim by the host of God and was comforted before he met his brother Esau (Gen. 32:22-31). And many weary ones still find that God's angelic messengers are round about them, so that they should not be left alone in the time of their trial.

The next thing that God did for Elijah, after He had allowed him to finish his journey and get to Horeb, was that He permitted him to tell his grief. You may have noticed that he told the story twice. He knew what he was grieving about, so he stated it very definitely—and the Lord allowed him to tell it. It is often a wonderful relief to be able to tell out your grief, to pull up the sluices and let the waters of sorrow run away. If no one but God shall hear it—if no human ear should listen to your complaining— yet it is a very sweet thing to unburden your heart. One hymn-writer says—"Bear and forbear, and silent be; Tell no man your misery"[7]—but I am not sure about the wisdom of that advice. At any rate, tell it to God, for He allowed His poor servant Elijah to pour out into His ear the sad tale of his woe.

This done, the Lord helped to restore His servant by revealing Himself, and revealing His ways to him. He made Elijah see that God is not so apparent in terrific agencies as in quieter forms, that He does not always accomplish

---

7.   Epictetus, *The Golden Sayings* http://classics.mit.edu/Epictetus/ goldsay.2.2.html (accessed April 7, 2015).

His purposes by earthquake and fire. The Lord let him see that "a still small voice" was being heard throughout Israel, although the Prophet thought that no good had come of his testimony. And thus he was cheered.

Next, the Lord gave him good news. He told Elijah that he still had 7,000 in Israel who had not bowed the knee to Baal—and that revelation still further cheered the Prophet's heart! Then the Lord did what perhaps was best of all for Elijah, he gave him some more work to do. He sent him off about his Master's business again and I guarantee you that when Elijah went back over that road, it was with a very different step from that which brought him down to Beersheba. He had come along terrified and distressed, but now he goes back with the majesty that belongs to the Tishbite—he is afraid of no Jezebel now! He calls out Elisha to be his successor and he denounces Ahab—and does it bravely and boldly—and no one hears of his wanting to hide away again! God had brought His servant up out of his depression, in the way I have described, and he never went back again to that sad condition.

What We Learn about our Desires to Die
Now I come to the practical conclusion of the matter which is this. Let us learn from Elijah's experience, first, that it is very seldom right for us to pray that we may die. It was not right for Elijah and it is very seldom right for anybody to do so. It is never right for any of you, whose death would be your eternal ruin, to wish to die. Perhaps I am addressing some unconverted people who, in their impatience against God, have wished to die. What would you have gained by death? That day would be all darkness and not light to you! It would devour you as stubble. For

any man to lay violent hands on himself in order to escape from trouble is the maddest of all actions! It is leaping into the fire to escape the sparks—casting yourself into Hell in order to avoid some temporary depression of spirit! Oh, if you are ever tempted in that way, God grant you Grace at once to say, "Get you behind me, Satan!" Even if you feel a desire to die in order to get out of this world of misery, crush it down. If you are an unconverted man, whatever the misery of this world is, it is nothing compared with the misery of the world to come! It is far better to bear the ills you have than to fly to others that you know not of—even common sense should teach you that.

As for the man of God, it is seldom, if ever, that he should get into such a state of heart as to wish for death. I know, Beloved, that we may sometimes very properly desire death. When we have had a more than usually clear sight of Christ, we have longed to be with Him. May not the bride desire to be perpetually in the Bridegroom's company? When sacred song has sometimes carried us on its bright wings of silver up into the clear atmosphere that is round about the gates of Heaven, we have wished to enter—we have longed that we might see our God. I have no doubt it is right enough, when we are wearied, to wish for the everlasting rest. When we are conscious of sin, it is right enough to wish to be where sin can never come and temptation can never more annoy. There must be such wishes. There must be such aspirations, for, to depart and to be with Christ is far better than to abide here (Phil. 1:23).

But we must never get into such a craving and longing for Heaven that we are not content to bide our time here. We do not like men who work for us to be always looking for

Saturday night to come. And there are some Christians who are always wanting their Saturday night to arrive. Be willing to do a good day's work, to do a good week's work, and then the Sabbath will be all the sweeter to you when you get up— "Where congregations ne'er break up, And Sabbaths have no end."[8] How long you and I are to be here, is no concern of ours. After all, we are not our own masters—we are our Lord's servants. If He thinks we can glorify Him better here than there, it must be our choice to remain here.

I remember a good woman, to whom the question was put when she was very sick, and very full of pain, "Do you wish to die or to live?" She answered, "I wish to have no wish about the matter, but to leave it in the hands of God." "But suppose the Lord Jesus Christ were to say to you, 'You are to have whichever you wish'? What would you choose?" She said, "I would ask Him to decide for me, but I would not like to have my choice." You see, if we were dying and we said, "This is our own choice," we should lack some comfort which we might otherwise have had. But when we feel, "It was no choice of ours, it was the choice of God that we should die," then it is sweet. And if you live, you can say, "I am not living now in answer to an impatient cry of mine—I am living because God willed it and there is a purpose to be served by it." And then it is sweet to live. So leave the matter alone, dear Friend, and let the Lord do as He wills with you.

Elijah wished to die and prayed an unwise prayer, but our blessed Master said to His Father, "Nevertheless, not as I will, but as You will," (Luke 22:42) and in all the throes

---

8.   J.G. Saxe, "The Model Church," (1872) http://www.pdmusic.org/towne/tmt72tmc.txt (accessed April 7, 2015).

of His death-agony, there was not a syllable of impatience, but a perfect resignation to the will of God. That is the first practical lesson.

And the second is that whenever we do wish to die, we must take care that it is from the very best of motives and that there is no selfishness in it—no wish to escape from suffering, or from service. We must wish to depart to be with Christ because it is far better—

> Let me be with You where You are,
> My Savior, my eternal rest!
> Then only will this longing heart
> Be fully and forever blest.[9]

And, lastly, there is one more practical lesson for us to learn—you and I have not the slightest idea of what is in store for us on earth. "Eye has not seen, nor ear heard, neither have entered into the heart of man, the things which God has prepared for them that love him" up yonder (1 Cor. 2:9)! And you do not know what He has prepared for you even here. Elijah says, "Let me die." But, Elijah, would you not like to live to veil your face in the Presence of God on Horeb? "Oh, yes!" he would say, "let me live till then." And, Elijah, would you not like to live to rebuke Ahab for his sin against Naboth? "Oh, yes! I should like to live till then." Would you not like to live till you have cast your mantle over that blessed servant of God, Elisha, who is to succeed you? "Oh, yes!" he would say, "let me live till then." And would you not like to live, Elijah, till you have seen the schools of the Prophets raised by your influence, which

---

9. Charlotte Elliot, http://bibletruthpublishers.com/charlotte-elliott/adrian-roach/the-little-flock-hymn-book-its-history-and-hymn-writers/a-roach/page-share/lxps-la-104952 (accessed April 7, 2015).

shall live, after both you and Elisha are gone, to keep alive the work of God? I think I hear the old man say, "Oh, yes! Let me live till then. Happy shall I be if I can see schools instituted for the training of ministers who shall go and preach in God's name. Yes, let me live till then!"

And you do not know, Brother, how much there is for you yet to live for. And you, my Sister, do not talk about dying, for you also have a great deal more to do before you get to Heaven-service for your Savior that will make Heaven all the better when you get there! God has such blessings in store for some of you that when they come to you, you will be like men that dream, and your mouth shall be filled with laughter, and your tongue with singing, and you will say, "The Lord has done great things for us; of which we are glad." Therefore, be of good courage and strengthen your hearts, and still wait upon the Lord until He comes. And may His blessing be with you forever! Amen.

5

The Man of Sorrows[1]

"A man of sorrows, and acquainted with grief."
(Isaiah 53:3)

Possibly a murmur will pass round the congregation, "This is a dreary subject and a mournful theme." But, O Beloved, it is not so, for great as were the woes of our Redeemer, they are all over now, and are to be looked back upon with sacred triumph! However severe the struggle, the victory has been won; the laboring vessel was severely tossed by

---

1. Charles Spurgeon, "The Man of Sorrows," *The Metropolitan Tabernacle Pulpit*, Sermon 1099. http://www.spurgeongems.org/vols19-21/chs1099.pdf, (accessed March 4, 2015).

the waves, but she has now entered into the desired haven. Our Savior is no longer in Gethsemane agonizing, or upon the Cross dying; the crown of thorns has been replaced by many crowns of Sovereignty; the nails and the spear have given way to the scepter.

Nor is this all, for though the suffering is ended, the blessed results never end. We may remember the travail, for the Man Child is born into the world. The sowing in tears is followed by a reaping in joy. The bruising of the heel of the woman's Seed is well recompensed by the breaking of the serpent's head. It is pleasant to hear of battles fought when a decisive victory has ended war and established peace. So that the double reflection that all the work of suffering is finished by the Redeemer, and that, from now on, He beholds the success of all His labors, we shall rejoice even while we enter into fellowship with His sufferings!

Let it never be forgotten that the subject of the sorrows of the Savior has proven to be more efficacious for comfort to mourners than any other theme in the compass of Revelation, or out of it. Even the glories of Christ afford no such consolation to afflicted spirits as the sufferings of Christ. Christ is in all attitudes the consolation of Israel, but He is most so as the Man of Sorrows. Troubled spirits turn not so much to Bethlehem as to Calvary; they prefer Gethsemane to Nazareth. The afflicted do not so much look for comfort in Christ as He will come a second time in splendor of state, as to Christ as He came the first time, a weary Man, and full of woes. The passion flower yields us the best perfume; the tree of the Cross bleeds the most healing balm; like in this case cures like, for there is no remedy for sorrow beneath the sun like the sorrows of

Immanuel. As Aaron's rod swallowed up all the other rods, so the griefs of Jesus make our griefs disappear, and thus you see that in the black soil of our subject, light is sown for the righteous; light which springs up for those who sit in darkness, and in the region of the shadow of death.

Let us go, then, without reluctance to the house of mourning, and commune with "The Chief Mourner," who above all others could say, "I am the Man who has seen affliction" (Lam. 3:1).

We will not stray from our Text this morning, but keep to it so closely as even to dwell upon each one of its words. The words shall give us our divisions—"A Man." "A Man of sorrows." "Acquainted with grief."

The Humanity of Jesus Our Help

There is no novelty to anyone here present in the Doctrine of the real and actual Manhood of the Lord Jesus Christ, but although there is nothing novel in it, there is everything *important* in it; therefore, let us hear it again. This is one of those Gospel Church bells which must be rung every Sunday; this is one of those provisions of the Lord's household, which, like bread and salt, should be put upon the table at every spiritual meal; this is the manna which must fall every day round about the camp. We can never meditate too much upon Christ's blessed Person as God and as Man. Let us reflect that He who is here called a Man was certainly "very God of very God" (Nicene Creed). "A Man," and "a Man of sorrows," and yet at the same time, "God over all, blessed forever" (Rom. 9:5). He who was "despised and rejected of men" (Isa. 53:3) was beloved and adored by angels! And He, from whom men hid their faces in contempt, was worshiped by cherubim and seraphim!

This is the great mystery of godliness. *God* was "manifest in the flesh" (1 Tim. 3:16). He who was God, and was in the beginning with God, was made flesh and dwelt among us! The Highest stooped to become the Lowest; the Greatest took His place among the least. Strange, and needing all our faith to grasp it, yet it is true that He who sat upon the well of Sychar, and said, "Give me to drink" (John 4:7), was none other than He who dug the channels of the ocean, and poured into them the floods! Son of Mary, You are also Son of Jehovah! Man of the substance of Your mother, You are also essential Deity! We worship You this day in spirit and in truth!

Remembering that Jesus Christ is God, it now behooves us to remember that His Manhood was nonetheless real and substantial. It differed from our own humanity in the absence of sin, but it differed in no other respect; it is idle to speculate upon a heavenly Manhood, as some have done, who have, by their very attempt at accuracy, been borne down by whirlpools of error! It is enough for us to know that the Lord was born of a woman, wrapped in swaddling bands, laid in a manger, and needed to be nursed by His mother as any other little child. He grew in stature like any other human being, and as a Man we know that He ate and drank, that He hungered and thirsted, rejoiced and sorrowed; His body could be touched and handled, wounded, and made to bleed. He was no phantom, but a Man of flesh and blood even as we are! He was a Man needing sleep, requiring food, and subject to pain; and a Man who, in the end yielded up His life to death. There may have been some distinction between His body and ours, for inasmuch as it was never defiled by sin, it was not capable of corruption. Otherwise in body and in soul, the

Lord Jesus was perfect Man after the order of our manhood, "Made in the likeness of sinful flesh" (Rom. 8:3), and we must think of Him under that aspect.

Our temptation is to regard the Lord's Humanity as something quite different from our own; we are apt to spiritualize it away, and not to think of Him as really bone of our bone, and flesh of our flesh. All this is akin to grievous error; we may fancy that we are honoring Christ by such conceptions, but Christ is never honored by that which is not true. He was a Man, a real Man, a Man of our race, the Son of Man. Indeed, He was a representative Man, the Second Adam—"As the children are partakers of flesh and blood, He also Himself took part of the same" (Heb. 2:14). "He made Himself of no reputation, and took upon Him the form of a Servant, and was made in the likeness of Man" (Phil. 2:7).

Jesus our Kin

Now this condescending participation in our Nature brings the Lord Jesus very near to us in relationship. Inasmuch as He was Man, though also God, He was, according to Hebrew Law, our *goel*—our kinsman, next of kin. Now it was according to the Law that if an inheritance had been lost, it was the right of the next of kin to redeem it. Our Lord Jesus exercised His legal right—seeing us sold into bondage, and our inheritance taken from us, He came forward to redeem both us and all our lost estate. A blessed thing it was for us that we had such a Kinsman! When Ruth went to glean in the fields of Boaz, it was the most gracious circumstance in her life that Boaz turned out to be her next of kin. And we who have gleaned in the fields of Mercy praise the Lord that His Only-Begotten

Son is the next of kin to us; He is our Brother, born for adversity. It would not have been consistent with Divine Justice for any other substitution to have been accepted for us, except that of a man. *Man* sinned, and man must make reparation for the injury done to the Divine Honor; the breach of the Law was caused by man, and by man must it be repaired; *man* had transgressed; man must be punished. It was not in the power of an angel to have said, "I will suffer for man"—for angelic sufferings would have made no amends for human sins. But the Man, the matchless Man, being the representative Man, and of right by kinship allowed to redeem, stepped in, suffered what was due, made amends to injured Justice, and thereby set us free! Glory be unto His blessed name!

And now, Beloved, since the Lord thus saw in Christ's Manhood a suitableness to become our Redeemer, I trust that many here who have been under bondage to Satan, will see in that same Human Nature an attraction leading them to approach Him. Sinner, you have not to come to an absolute God; you are not bid to draw near to the Consuming Fire; you might well tremble to approach Him whom you have so grievously offended. But there is a Man ordained to mediate between you and God, and if you would come to God, you must come *through* Him—the Man Christ Jesus. God out of Christ is terrible out of His Holy places; He will by no means spare the guilty—but look at yonder Son of Man!—

"His hand no thunder bears, No terror clothes His brow;
No bolts to drive your guilty souls to fiercer flames below!"[2]

2.   Isaac Watts, "The Psalms and Hymns of Isaac Watts II," Hymn 104 (1806)
     (www.hymnary.org/hymn/PHW/II.104), accessed March 21, 2015.

He is a Man with hands full of blessing, eyes wet with tears of pity, lips overflowing with Love, and a heart melting with tenderness! See you not the gash in His side? Through that wound there is a highway to His heart, and he who needs His Compassion may soon excite it! O Sinners, the way to the Savior's heart is open, and penitent seekers shall never be denied! Why should the most despairing be afraid to approach the Savior? He has deigned to assume the Character of the Lamb of God—I have never known even a little child who was afraid of a lamb! The most timorous will approach a lamb, and Jesus used this argument when He said to every laboring and heavy-laden one, "Take My yoke upon you, and learn of Me, for I am meek and lowly in heart" (Matt. 11:29).

We Touch Jesus's Sympathy

I know you feel yourselves sad and trembling, but need you tremble in His Presence? If you are weak, your weakness will touch His Sympathy, and your mournful inability will be an argument with His boundless Mercy! If I were sick and might have my choice where I would lie, with a view to healing, I would say, "Place me where the best and kindest physician upon earth can see me! Put me where a man with great skill and equal tenderness will have me always beneath his eyes; I shall not long groan there in vain; if he can heal me he will." Sinner, place yourself, by an act of faith, beneath the Cross of Jesus! Look up to Him, and say, "Blessed Physician, You whose wounds for me can heal me; whose death for me can make me live; look down upon me! You are Man; You know what man suffers! You are Man; will You let a man sink down to Hell who cries to You for help? You are a Man, and You can save, and will

97

You let a poor unworthy one who longs for Your Mercy be driven into hopeless misery while he cries to You to let Your merits save him?" Oh, you guilty ones, have faith that you can reach the heart of Jesus! Sinner, fly to Jesus without fear! He waits to save! It is His Office to receive sinners, and reconcile them to God; be thankful that you have not to go to God at the first, and as you are, but you are invited to come to Jesus Christ, and *through Him* to the Father! May the Holy Spirit lead you to devout meditation upon the humility of our Lord, and so may you find the door of life, the portal of peace, the gate of Heaven!

Then let me add, before I leave this point, that every child of God ought also to be comforted by the fact that our Redeemer is one of our own race, seeing that He was made like unto His brethren, that He might be a merciful and faithful High Priest; and He was tempted in all points, like as we are, that He might be able to succor them who are tempted (Heb. 4:15). The sympathy of Jesus is the next most precious thing to His Sacrifice. I stood by the bedside of a Christian Brother the other day, and he remarked, "I feel thankful to God that our Lord took our sicknesses." "Of course," said he, "the grand thing was that He took our sins, but next to that, I, as a sufferer, feel grateful that He also took our sicknesses." Personally, I also bear witness that it has been to me, in seasons of great pain, superlatively comfortable to know that in every pang which racks His people, the Lord Jesus has a fellow feeling! We are not alone, for one like unto the Son of Man walks the furnace with us! The clouds which float over our sky have aforetime darkened the heavens for Him, also—

"He knows what temptations mean, for He has felt the same" (Heb. 2:18).

How completely it takes the bitterness out of grief to know that it once was suffered by Jesus! The Macedonian soldiers, it is said, made long forced marches which seemed to be beyond the power of mortal endurance; but the reason for their untiring energy lay in Alexander's *presence*; he was accustomed to walk with them, and bear the same fatigue. If the king himself had been calcified like a Persian monarch in a palanquin in the midst of easy, luxurious state, the soldiers would soon have grown tired; but when they looked upon the king of men himself, hungering when they hungered, thirsting when they thirsted, often putting aside the cup of water offered to him, and passing it to a fellow soldier who looked more faint than himself, they could not dream of repining! Why, every Macedonian felt that he could endure any fatigue if Alexander could! This day, assuredly, we can bear poverty, slander, contempt, or bodily pain—death itself—because Jesus Christ our Lord has borne it! By His humiliation it shall become pleasure to be abased for His sake! By the spit that ran down His cheeks, it shall become a fair thing to be made a mockery for Him! By the buffeting and the blindfolding it shall become an honor to be disgraced, and by the Cross it shall become life itself, to surrender life for the sake of such a cause, and so precious a Master! May the Man of Sorrows now appear to us, and enable us to bear our sorrows cheerfully! If there is consolation anywhere, surely it is to be found in the delightful Presence of the Crucified—"A Man shall be a hiding place from the wind, and a covert from the tempest" (Isa. 32:2).

The Sorrow of Jesus

We must pass on to dwell for a while upon the next words, "a man of sorrows." The expression is intended to be very emphatic. It is not, "A sorrowful Man," but, "A Man of sorrows," as if He was made up of sorrows, and they were constituent elements of His Being. Some are men of pleasure, others men of wealth, but He was "A Man of sorrows." He and sorrow might have changed names. He who saw Him, saw sorrow, and he who would see sorrow, must look on Him. "Behold, and see," He says, "if there was ever sorrow like unto My sorrow which was done unto Me" (Lam. 1:12).

Our Lord is called the Man of Sorrows for *peculiarity*, for this was His peculiar token and special mark. We might well call Him, "A Man of Holiness," for there was no fault in Him; or "A Man of labors," for He did His Father's business earnestly; or, "A Man of eloquence," for never a man spoke like this Man! We might right fittingly call Him in the language of our hymn, "The Man of Love," for never was there greater love than glowed in His heart! Still, conspicuous as all these, and many other excellencies were, yet had we gazed upon Christ, and been asked afterwards what was the most striking peculiarity in Him, we should have said His sorrows. The various parts of His Character were so singularly harmonious that no one quality predominated so as to become a leading feature. In His moral portrait, the eyes are perfect, but so is the mouth; the cheeks are as beds of spices, but the lips are as lilies, dropping sweet-smelling myrrh!

In Peter you see enthusiasm exaggerated at times into presumption; and in John, love for his Lord would call fire from Heaven on his foes. Deficiencies and exaggerations exist everywhere but in Jesus! He is the *perfect* Man, a whole Man, and the Holy One of Israel. But there was a peculiarity, and it lay in the fact that "His visage was so marred more than any man, and His form more than the sons of men" (Isa. 52:14), through the excessive griefs which continually passed over His spirit. Tears were His insignia, and the Cross His escutcheon! He was the chief warrior in black armor, and not as now, the rider upon the white horse. He was the Lord of Grief, the Prince of Pain, the Emperor of Anguish, a "Man of Sorrows, and acquainted with grief."—

> "Oh! King of Grief! (A title strange, yet true,
> To You of all kings only due),
> Oh! King of Wounds! How shall I grieve for Thee,
> Who in all grief prevents me?"[3]

Is not the title, "Man of Sorrows," given to our Lord by way of eminence? He was not only sorrowful, but pre-eminent among the sorrowful! All men have a burden to bear, but His was heaviest of all! Who is there of our race that is quite free from sorrows? Search the whole earth through, and the thorn and thistle will be found everywhere; and these have wounded everyone born of woman. High in the lofty places of the earth there is sorrow, for the royal widow weeps her lord. Down in the cottage where we fancy that nothing but content can reign, a thousand bitter tears are shed over dire penury and cruel oppression. In the sunniest climates the serpent creeps among the flowers; in the most fertile regions poisons flourish as well as wholesome herbs;

---

3.   George Herbert, "The Thanksgiving," *The Poetical Works of George Herbert and Reginald Heber: With Memoirs. Eight Engravings on Steel* (Gall & Inglis 1861), p. 25.

everywhere, "Men must work and women must weep."[4] There is sorrow on the sea, and sadness on the land, but in this common lot, the "firstborn among many brethren" (Rom. 8:29) has more than a double portion! His cup is bitterer; His Baptism is deeper than the rest of the family! Common sufferers must give place, for none can match with Him in woe! Ordinary mourners may be content to tear their garments, but *He* is torn in His affliction; they sip at Sorrow's bowl, but He drains it dry; He who was the most obedient Son smarted most under the rod when He was stricken of God and afflicted! No other of the smitten ones have sweat great drops of blood, or in the same bitterness of anguish, cried, "My God, My God, why have You forsaken Me?" (Matt. 27:46).

The Pains and Tenderness of Jesus

The reasons for this superior sorrow may be found in the fact that with His sorrow there was no mixture of sin. Sin deserves sorrow, but it also blunts the edge of grief by rendering the soul untender and unsympathetic. We do not start at sin as Jesus did; we do not tremble at the sinner's doom as Jesus would. His was a perfect Nature which, because it knew no sin, was not in its element amid sorrow, but was like a land bird driven out to sea by the gale. To the robber, jail is his home, and the prison fare is the meat to which he is accustomed; but to an innocent man a prison is misery, and everything about it is strange and foreign. Our Lord's pure Nature was peculiarly sensitive of any contact with sin. We, alas, by the Fall have lost

---

4.   Charles Kingsley, "The Three Fishers," in Stedman, Edmund Clarence, ed. A Victorian Anthology 1837-1895. (Cambridge: Riverside Press, 1895), www.bartleby.com/246/, accessed March 21, 2015.

much of that feeling! In proportion as we are sanctified, sin becomes the source of wretchedness to us. Jesus, being Perfect every sin pained Him much more than it would any of us.

I have no doubt there are many persons in the world who could live merrily in the haunts of vice—could hear blasphemy without horror, view lust without disgust, and look on robbery or murder without abhorrence. But to many of us, an hour's familiarity with such abominations would be the severest punishment; a sentence in which the name of Jesus is blasphemed is torture to us of the most exquisite kind; the very mention of the shameful deeds of vice seizes us with horror; to live with the wicked would be a sufficient Hell to the righteous. David's prayer is full of agony where he cries, "Gather not my soul with sinners, nor my life with bloody men" (Ps. 26:9). But the Perfect Jesus! What a grief the sight of sin must have caused Him! Our hands grow rough with toiling, and our hearts with sinning—but our Lord was, as it were, like a man whose flesh was all one quivering wound; He was delicately sensitive of every touch of sin. We go through thorn brakes and briars of sin because we are clothed with indifference, but imagine a naked man, compelled to traverse a forest of briars; such was the Savior as to His moral sensitiveness; He could see sin where we cannot see it, and feel its heinousness as we cannot feel it. There was, therefore, more to grieve Him, and He was more capable of being grieved.

Side by side with His painful sensitiveness of the evil of sin was His gracious tenderness towards the sorrows of others. If we could know and enter into all the griefs of this congregation, it is probable that we would be of all men, most miserable. There are heartbreaks in this house this morning, which, could they find a tongue, would fill our heart with agony! We hear of poverty here, we see disease there, we observe bereavement, and we mark distress. We note the fact that men are passing into the grave, and (ah, far more bitter grief), descending into Hell! But, somehow or other, either these become such common things that they do not stir us, or else we gradually harden to them. The Savior was always moved to sympathy with another's griefs, for His Love was always at flood-tide. All men's sorrows were His sorrows; His heart was so large that it was inevitable that He should become "a Man of sorrows."

We remember that besides this, our Savior had a peculiar relationship to sin. He was not merely afflicted with the sight of it, and saddened by perceiving its effects on others, but sin was actually laid upon Him, and He was numbered with the transgressors, and therefore He was called to bear the terrible blows of Divine Justice, and suffered unknown, immeasurable agonies! His Godhead strengthened Him to suffer, else mere Manhood had failed. The Wrath whose power no man knows spent itself on Him— "It pleased the Father to bruise Him, He has put Him to grief" (Isa. 53:10). Behold the Man, and marvel how vain it would be to seek His equal sorrow!

The title of "Man of Sorrows," was also given to our Lord to indicate the *constancy* of His afflictions. He changed His place of abode, but He always lodged with Sorrow. Sorrow wove His swaddling bands, and Sorrow His winding sheet. Born in a stable, Sorrow received Him, and only on the Cross at His last breath did Sorrow part with Him! His disciples might forsake Him, but His Sorrow would not leave Him; He was often alone without a man, but never alone without a grief. From the hour of His Baptism in Jordan, to the time of His Baptism in the pains of death, He always wore the sable robe, and was "a Man of sorrows."

Sorrows of Body and Soul

He was also "a Man of sorrows," for the *variety* of His woes. He was a Man not of sorrow, only, but of "sorrows." All the sufferings of the body and of the soul were known to Him. The sorrows of the man who actively struggles to obey; the sorrows of the man who sits still, and passively endures; the sorrows of the lofty He knew, for He was the King of Israel. The sorrows of the poor He knew, for He "had nowhere to lay his head" (Matt. 8:20). Sorrows relative, and sorrows personal; sorrows mental, and sorrows spiritual. Sorrows of all kinds and degrees assailed Him! Affliction emptied his quiver upon Him, making His heart the target for all conceivable woes. Let us think a minute or two of some of those sufferings.

Our Lord was a Man of sorrows as to His poverty. Oh, you who are in need, your need is not so abject as His—He had nowhere to lay His head, but you have at least some humble roof to shelter you! No one denies you a cup of water, but He sat upon the well at Samaria, and said, "I thirst." We read more than once that He hungered; His toil was so great that He was constantly weary, and we read of one occasion where they took Him, "Even as He was," into the boat—too faint was He to reach the boat Himself, but they carried Him as He was, and laid Him down near the helm to sleep. But He had not much time for slumber, for they woke Him, saying, "Master, do You not care that we perish?" (Mark 4:38). A hard life was His, with nothing of earthly comfort to make that life endurable! Remember, you who lament around the open grave, or weep in memory of graves newly filled—our Savior knew the heart-rending of bereavement. Jesus wept as He stood at the tomb of Lazarus.

Perhaps the bitterest of His sorrows were those which were connected with His gracious work. He came as the Messiah sent of God on a mission of Love, and men rejected His claims. When He went to His own city where He had been brought up, and announced Himself, they would have cast Him headlong from the brow of the hill! It is a hard thing to come on an errand of disinterested Love, and then to meet with such ingratitude as that. Nor did they stop at cold rejection; they then proceeded to derision and to ridicule. There was no name of contempt which they did not pour upon Him. No, it was not merely contempt, but they proceeded to lies, slander, and blasphemy. He was a drunk, they said—hear this, you angels, and be astonished! Yes, a wine-bibber did they call the blessed Prince of Life! They said He was in league with Beelzebub, and had a devil, and was mad—whereas He had come to destroy the works of the devil!! They charged Him with every crime which their malice could suggest; there was not a word He spoke but they would twist it; not a Doctrine but what they would misrepresent it. He could not speak but what they would find in His words some occasion against Him, and all the while He was doing nothing but seeking their advantage in all ways! When He was earnest against their vices, it was out of pity for their souls; if He condemned their sins, it was because their sins would destroy them; but His zeal against sin was always tempered with His Love for the souls of men. Was there ever Man so full of goodwill to others who received such disgraceful treatment from those He longed to serve?

Jesus's Sorrows Multiplied

As He proceeded in His life, His sorrows multiplied; He preached, and when men's hearts were hard, and they would not believe what He said, "He was grieved for the hardness of their hearts" (Mark 3:5). He went about doing good, and for His good works they took up stones to stone Him! Alas, they stoned His heart when they could not injure His body. He pleaded with them, and plaintively declared His Love, and received, instead thereof, a remorseless and fiendish hatred! Slighted love has griefs of peculiar poignancy—many have died of hearts broken by ingratitude. Such love as the Love of Jesus could not, for the sake of those it loved, bear to be slighted; it pined within itself because men did not know their own mercies, and rejected their own Salvation! His sorrow was not that men injured Him, but that they destroyed themselves! This it was that pulled up the sluices of His Soul, and made His eyes overflow with tears—"O Jerusalem! Jerusalem! How often would I have gathered your children together as a hen gathers her chickens under her wings, and you would not" (Matt. 23:37). The lament is not for His own humiliation, but for their suicidal rejection of His Divine Grace! These were among the sorrows that He bore.

But surely He found some solace with the few companions whom He had gathered around Him. He did, but for all that He must have found as much sorrow as solace in their company; they were dull scholars, they learned slowly; what they did learn they forgot; what they remembered they did not practice, and what they practiced at one time, they belied at another! They were miserable comforters for the Man of Sorrows. His was a lonely life; I mean that even when He was with His followers He was alone. He said to them once, "Could you not watch with Me one hour" (Matt. 26:40), but, indeed, He might have said the same to them all the hours of their lives, for even if they sympathized with Him to the utmost of their capacity, they could not enter into such griefs as His! A father in a house with many little children about him cannot tell his babes his griefs; if he did they would not comprehend him. What do they know of his anxious business transactions, or his crushing losses? Poor little things, their father does not wish they should be able to sympathize with him; he looks down upon them, and rejoices that their toys will comfort them, and that their little prattle will not be broken in upon by his great griefs.

The Savior, from the very dignity of His Nature, must suffer alone; the mountainside with Christ upon it seems to me to be a suggestive symbol of His earthly life. His great soul lived in vast solitudes, sublime and terrible, and there, amid a midnight of trouble, His Spirit communed with the Father, no one being able to accompany Him into the dark glens and gloomy ravines of His unique experience. Of all His life's warfare, He might have said in some senses, "Of the people there was none with Me" (Isa. 63:3) and at the last it became literally true, for they all forsook Him; one denied Him, and another betrayed Him, so that He trod the winepress alone.

In the last crowning sorrows of His life, there came upon Him the penal inflictions from God—the punishment of our sin which was upon Him. He was arrested in the garden of Gethsemane by God's officers before the officers of the Jews had come near to Him! There on the ground He knelt and wrestled till the bloody sweat poured from every pore and His soul was "exceedingly sorrowful, even unto death" (Matt. 26:38). You have read the story of your Master's woes, and know how He was hurried from bar to bar, and treated with mingled scorn and cruelty before each judgment seat. When they had taken Him to Herod and to Pilate, and almost murdered Him with scourging, they brought Him forth and said, *Ecce Homo*—"Behold the Man" (John 19:5). Their malice was not satisfied; they must go further, and nail Him to His Cross, and mock Him while fever parched His mouth and made Him feel as if His body were dissolved to dust. He cries out, "I thirst" (John 19:28), and is mocked with vinegar! You know the rest, but I would have you best remember that the sharpest scourging and severest griefs were all *within*—while the hand of God bruised Him, and the iron rod of Justice broke Him, as it were, upon the wheel.

He was fitly named a "Man of Sorrows!" I feel as if I have no utterance, as if my tongue were tied while trying to speak upon this subject. I cannot find goodly words worthy of my theme, yet I know that embellishments of language would degrade rather than adorn the agonies of my Lord. There let the Cross stand sublime in its simplicity! It needs no decoration! If I had wreaths of choicest flowers to hang about it, I would gladly place them there, and if instead of garlands of flowers, each flower could be a priceless gem, I would consider that the Cross deserved the whole; but as I have none of these, I rejoice that the Cross, alone, in its naked simplicity, needs nothing from mortal speech. Turn to your bleeding Savior, O my Hearers. Continue gazing upon Him, and find in the "Man of Sorrows" your Lord and your God!

Jesus Acquainted with Grief

And now the last word is, He was "acquainted with grief." With grief He had an *intimate* acquaintance! He did not know merely what it was in others, but it came home to Him. We have read of grief. We have sympathized with grief; we have sometimes felt grief—but the Lord felt it more intensely than other men in His innermost soul; He, beyond us all, was conversant with this black letter lore; He knew the secret of the heart which refuses to be comforted; He had sat at Grief's table, eaten of Grief's black bread, and dipped His morsel in her vinegar. By the waters of Marah He dwelt and knew right well the bitter well. He and Grief were bosom friends.

It was a *continuous* acquaintance. He did not call at Grief's house, sometimes, to take a tonic by the way. Neither did He sip, now and then, of the wormwood and the gall, but the quassia cup was *always* in His hand, ashes were always mingled with His bread. Not only forty days in the wilderness did Jesus fast; the world was always a wilderness to Him, and His life was one long Lent. I do not say that He was not, after all, a happy Man, for down deep in His soul, benevolence always supplied a living spring of joy to Him. There was a joy into which we are one day to enter—the "Joy of our Lord"—the "Joy set before Him" for which "He endured the Cross, despising the shame" (Heb. 12:2). But that does not at all take away from the fact that His acquaintance with Grief was continuous and intimate beyond that of any man who ever lived! It was, indeed, a growing acquaintance with Grief, for each step took Him deeper down into the grim shades of sorrow. As there is a progress in the teaching of Christ, and in the life of Christ, so is there in the griefs of Christ. The tempest

[handwritten margin note: bitter tonic]

lowered darker, and darker, and darker; His sun rose in a cloud, but it set in congregated horrors of heaped up night, till, in a moment, the clouds were suddenly torn in sunder, and as a loud Voice proclaimed, "It is finished" (John 19:30), a glorious morning dawned where all expected an eternal night!

Remember, once more, that this acquaintance of Christ with Grief was a *voluntary* acquaintance for our sakes. He need never have known Grief at all, and at any moment He might have said to Grief, "Farewell!" He could have returned in an instant to the royalties of Heaven, and to the bliss of the upper world, or even tarrying here He might have lived sublimely indifferent to the woes of mankind. But He would not—He remained to the end, out of His Love to us—Grief's acquaintance!

Saturated With Jesus

Now, then, what shall I say in conclusion, but just this: let us admire the superlative Love of Jesus. O Love, Love, what have You done? What have You *not* done? You are Omnipotent in suffering! Few of us can bear pain; perhaps fewer still of us can bear misrepresentation, slander, and ingratitude. These are horrible hornets which sting as with fire; men have been driven to madness by cruel scandals which have distilled from venomous tongues. Christ, throughout life, bore these and other sufferings! Let us love Him, as we think of how much He must have loved us! Will you try, this afternoon, before you come to the Communion Table, to get your souls saturated with the Love of Christ? Soak them in His Love all afternoon, till, like a sponge, you drink into your own selves the Love of Jesus! And then come up tonight, as it were, to let that Love flow out to Him again while you sit at His Table, and partake of the emblems of His death and of His Love. Admire the power of His Love, and then pray that you may have a love somewhat akin to it in power. We sometimes wonder why the Church of God grows so slowly, but I do not wonder when I remember what scant consecration to Christ there is in the Church of God. Jesus was "a Man of sorrows, and acquainted with grief," but many of His disciples who profess to be altogether His, are living for themselves! There are rich men who call themselves saints, and are thought to be so, whose treasures are hoarded for themselves and families! There are men of ability who believe that they are bought with Christ's blood, yet their ability is all spent on other things, and none upon their Lord!

And let us come nearer home—here are we, what are we doing? Teaching in the school, are you? Are you doing it with all your heart *for Jesus*? Preaching in the street? Yes, but do you throw your soul into it for *Him*? Maybe you have to confess you are doing nothing—do not let this day conclude till you have begun to do something for your Lord! We are always talking about the Church doing this, and doing that—what is the Church? I believe there is a great deal too much said, both of bad and good, about that abstraction. The fact is, we are *individuals!* The church is only the aggregation of *individuals*, and if any good is to be done it must be performed by *individuals!* And if all individuals are idle, there is no church work done! There may be the semblance of it, but there is no real work done! Brothers and Sisters, what are you *doing for Jesus?* I charge you by the nail-prints of His hands, unless you are a liar unto Him, LABOR for Him! I charge you by His wounded feet—run to His help! I charge you by the scar on His side—give Him your heart! I charge you by that sacred head once pierced with thorns—yield Him your thoughts! I charge you by the shoulders which bore the scourges—bend your whole strength to His service! I charge you by Himself give Him yourself! I charge you by that left hand which has been under your head, and that right hand which has embraced you, by the roes and by the hinds of the field, by the beds of spices, and the banquets of love, render yourself, your heart, your soul, your strength to Him! Live in His service, and die in His service! Lay not down your harness, but work on as long as you shall live. While you live let this be your motto— "All for Jesus, all for Jesus; all for the Man of Sorrows, all for the Man of Sorrows!"

O you that love Him and fight for Him, you are summoned to the front! Hasten to the conflict, I pray you, and charge home for the "Man of Sorrows!" Make this your battle cry today! Slink not back like cowards! Flee not to your homes as lovers of ease, but press to the front for the "Man of Sorrows," like good men, and true. By the Cross which bore Him, and by the heavy Cross He bore; by His death agony, and by the agony of His life, I cry, "Forward, for the Man of Sorrows!" Write this word, "For the Man of Sorrows," on your own bodies, wherein you bear the marks of the Lord Jesus! Brand, if not in your flesh, yet in your souls, for from now on you are servants of the Man of Sorrows! Write this on your wealth! Bind this inscription on all your possessions—"This belongs to the Man of Sorrows." Give your children to the "Man of Sorrows," as men of old consecrated their sons to patriotism, and to battle with their country's foes! Give up each hour to the

"Man of Sorrows!" Learn, even, to eat and drink, and sleep for the "Man of Sorrows," doing all in His name. Live for Him, and be ready to die for Him, and the Lord accept you for the "Man of Sorrows' " sake. Amen.

6

Healing for the Wounded[1]

*"He heals the broken in heart and binds up
their wounds."
(Psalm 147:3)*

Perhaps there is nothing which gives us a nobler view of
the greatness of God than a contemplation of the starry
heavens, when by night we lift up our eyes and behold
Him who has created all these things. When we remember
that He brings out their host by number, calls them all by
their names and that by the greatness of His power not
one fails, then, indeed, we adore a mighty God and our

---

1.   Charles Spurgeon, "Healing for the Wounded," *The New Park Street Pulpit*, Sermon 53. http://www.spurgeongems.org/vols1-3/chs53.pdf, (accessed March 4, 2015).

soul naturally falls prostrate in reverential awe before the throne of Him who leads the host of Heaven and marshals the stars in their armies!

But the Psalmist has here placed another fact side by side with this wondrous act of God. He declares that the same God who leads the stars, who tells the number of them, and calls them by their names, heals the broken in heart and binds up their wounds!

The next time you rise to some idea of God by viewing the starry floor of His magnificent temple above, strive to compel your contemplation to this thought—that the same mighty hand which rolls the stars along, puts liniments around the wounded heart—that the same Being who spoke the worlds into existence and now impels those ponderous globes through their orbits, does, in His mercy, cheer the wounded and heal the broken in heart!

We will not delay you by a preface, but will come at once to the two thoughts. First, here is a *great ill*—a broken heart. And secondly, a *great mercy*—"*He heals* the broken in heart and binds up their wounds."

We are Double Beings

Man is a double being—he is composed of body and soul—and each of the portions of man may receive injury and hurt. The wounds of the body are extremely painful and if they amount to a breaking of the frame, the torture is singularly exquisite. Yet God has, in His mercy, provided means whereby wounds may be healed and injuries repaired. The soldier who retires from the battlefield knows that he shall find a hand to extricate the shot and certain ointments and liniments to heal his wounds.

We very speedily care for bodily diseases. They are too painful to let us slumber in silence and they soon urge us to seek a physician or a surgeon for our healing. Oh, if only we were as much alive to the more serious wounds of our *inner man!* If we were as deeply sensible of *spiritual* injuries, how earnestly would we cry to "the beloved physician"— and how soon would we prove His power to save! Stabbed in the most vital part by the hand of our original parent and, from head to foot disabled by our own sin, we yet remain as insensible as steel—careless and unmoved—because though our wounds are known, they are not felt!

We would count that soldier foolish who would be more anxious to repair a broken helmet than an injured limb. Are not we even more to be condemned when we give precedence to the perishing fabric of the body and neglect the immortal soul? You, however, who have *broken hearts,* can no longer be insensible. You have felt *too acutely* to slumber in indifference! Your bleeding spirit cries for consolation—may my glorious *Master* give me words in season for you! We intend to address you upon the important subject of broken hearts and the great healing provided for them.

Natural Reasons for a Broken Heart

Let us commence with the great ill—a broken heart. What is it? We reply there are several forms of a broken heart. Some are what we call naturally broken and some are spiritually so. We will occupy a moment by mentioning certain forms of this evil, naturally considered. And verily our task would be a dreary one if we were called upon to witness one tenth of the misery endured by those who suffer from a broken heart!

There have been hearts broken by *desertion*. A wife has been neglected by a husband who was once the subject of her attachment and whom even now she tenderly loves. Scorned and despised by the man who once lavished upon her every token of his affection, she has known what a broken heart means. A friend is forsaken by one upon whom he leaned, to whose very soul he was knit, so that their two hearts had grown into one. He feels that his heart is broken, for the other half of himself is severed from him. When Ahithophel forsakes David, when the kind friend unto whom we have always told our sorrows, betrays our confidence, the consequence may possibly be a broken heart. The desertion of a man by his fellows, the ingratitude of children to their parents, the unkindness of parents to their children, the betrayal of secrets by a comrade, the changeableness and fickleness of friends— along with other modes of desertion which happen in this world—have brought about broken hearts. We know not a more fruitful source of broken hearts than disappointment in the objects of our affections—to find that we have been deceived where we have placed our confidence. It is not simply that we leaned upon a broken reed and the reed has snapped—that were bad enough—but in the fall, we fell upon a thorn which pierced our heart to its center! Many have there been who have gone to their graves not smitten by disease, not slain by the sword—but with a far direr wound than the sword could ever give, a more desperate death than poison could ever cause! May you never know such agony!

We have also seen hearts broken by *bereavement*. We have known tender wives who have laid their husbands in the tomb and who have stood by the grave until their very heart did break for solitary anguish. We have seen parents bereaved of their beloved offspring, one after another. And when they have been called to hear the solemn words, "earth to earth, dust to dust, ashes to ashes," over the last of their children, they have turned away from the grave, bidding adieu—longing for death and abhorring life! To such the world becomes a prison—cheerless, cold, and unutterably miserable. The owl and bittern seem, alone, to sympathize with them and anything of joy in the whole world appears to be but, intended, as a mockery to their misery. Divine grace, however, can sustain them even here!

How frequently might this be supposed to occur to our brave countrymen engaged in the present war? Do not they feel, and acutely feel, the loss of their comrades? You will, perhaps, imagine that the slaughter and death around them prevent the tender feelings of nature. You are enough mistaken if you so dream! The soldier's heart may never know fear, but it has not forgotten sympathy! The fearful struggle around renders it impossible to pay the usual court and homage at the gates of sorrow, but there is more of real grief, oftentimes, in the hurried midnight funeral than in the flaunting pageantry of your pompous processions. Were it in our power to walk among the tents, we would find abundant need to use the words of our text by way of cordial to many a warrior who has seen all his chosen companions fall before the destroyer!

Oh you mourners! You who seek a balm for your wounds—let me proclaim it unto you—you are not ignorant of it, I trust, but let me apply that in which you already place your confidence. The God of Heaven knows your sorrows, repair to His throne and tell your simple tale of woe! Then cast your burden on *Him*. He will bear it!

Open your heart before *Him*—He will heal it! Think not that you are beyond hope. You would be if there were no God of love and pity, but while Jehovah lives, the mourner need not despair!

Poverty has also contributed its share to the number of the army of misery. Pinching need, a noble desire to walk erect without the crutch of charity, and inability to obtain employment have, at times, driven men to desperate measures. Many a goodly cedar has withered for lack of moisture and so has many a man pined away beneath the deprivations of extreme poverty. Those who are blessed with sufficiency can scarcely guess the pain endured by the sons of need—especially if they have once been rich. Yet O child of suffering, be patient—God has not passed you over in His Providence. Feeder of sparrows, He will also furnish *you* with what you need! Sit not down in despair—hope on, always hope! Take up arms against a sea of troubles and your opposition shall yet end your distresses. *There is* one who cares for you. One eye is fixed on you, even in the home of your destitution. One heart beats with pity for your woes and an omnipotent hand shall yet stretch out to you the needed help! The dark cloud shall yet scatter itself in its season—the blackest gloom shall have its morning! *He* will bind up your wounds, and heal your broken heart with hands of grace if you are one of His family!

Multiplied also are the cases where *disappointment* and *defeat* have crushed the spirits. The soldier fighting for his country may see the ranks broken, but he will not be broken in heart as long as there remains a single hope for victory. His comrade reels behind him and he, himself, is wounded, but with a shout, he cries, "On! On!" and scales the ramparts. Sword in hand, he still goes carrying terror among the foe, himself sustained by the prospect of victory. But let him once hear the shout of defeat where he hoped for triumph. Let him know that the banner is stained in the earth, that the eagle has been snatched from the standard. Let him once hear it said, "They fly, they fly!" Let him see the officers and soldiers flying in confusion—let him be well assured that the most heroic courage and the most desperate valor are of no use—then his heart bursts under a sense of dishonor! Then he is almost content to die because the honor of his country has been tarnished and her glory has been stained in the dust. Of this the soldiers of Britain know but little—may they speedily carve out a peace for us with their victorious swords! Truly in the great conflict of life we can bear anything but defeat. Toils on toils would we endure to climb a summit, but if we must die before we reached it—that were a brokenness of heart, indeed! To accomplish the objective on which we have set our minds, we would spend our very heart's blood. But once let us see that our life's purpose is not to be accomplished—let us, when we hoped to grasp the crown, see that it is withdrawn, or other hands have seized it—then comes brokenness of heart. But let us remember, whether we have been broken in heart by poverty or by defeat, that there is a hand which "binds up the broken in heart and heals all their wounds" (Ps. 147:3).

Even these natural breakings are regarded by Jehovah, who, in the plentitude of His mercy, gives a balm for every wound to each of His people! We need not ask, "Is there no balm in Gilead? Is there no physician there?" (Jer. 8:22). There *is* a balm! There *is* a Physician who can heal all these natural wounds, who can give joy to the troubled countenance, take the furrow from the brow, wipe the tear from the eyes, remove the agitation from the bosom—and calm the heart now swelling with grief. He "heals the broken in heart and binds up their wounds" (Ps. 147:3).

Spiritual Reasons for a Broken Heart

But all that we have mentioned of woe and sorrow which the natural heart endures is not sufficient to explain our text. The heart broken not by distress or disappointment, but on account of *sin*, is the heart which God peculiarly delights to heal. All other sufferings may find a fearful center in one breast, and yet the subject of them may be unpardoned and unsaved. But if the heart is broken for sin by the Holy Spirit, salvation will be its ultimate issue and Heaven its result! At the time of regeneration, the soul is subject to an inward work, causing considerable suffering at the time. This suffering does not continue after the soul has learned the preciousness of a Savior's blood, but while it lasts, it produces an effect which is never forgotten in later life! Let none suppose that the pains we are about to describe are the constant companions of an heir of Heaven during his entire existence. They are like the torture of a great drunkard at the time of his reformation, rendered necessary, not by the reformation, but by his old habits. So this broken heart is felt at the time of that change of which the Bible speaks, when it says, "Except a man be born again, he cannot see the kingdom of God" (John 3:3). The fruit of the Spirit is afterwards joy and peace, but for a season we must, if saved, endure much mental agony.

Are any of you at the present moment disturbed in mind and vexed in spirit because you have violated the commands of God? And are you anxious to know whether these feelings are tokens of genuine brokenness and contrition? Hear me, then, while I briefly furnish you with tests whereby you may discern the truth and value of your repentance.

1. We cannot conceive it possible that you are broken in heart if the pleasures of the world are your delight. We may consent to call you amiable, estimable and honorable, even, should you mix somewhat in the amusements of life—but it would be a treason to your common sense to tell you that such things are consistent with a broken heart! Will any venture to assert that yon gay reveler has a broken heart? Would he not consider it an insult, should you suggest it? Does that lewd song, now defiling the air, proceed from the lips of a broken-hearted sinner? Can the fountain, when filled with sorrow, send forth such streams as these? No, my friends, the wanton, the lewd, the rioting and the profane are too wise to lay claim to the title of broken-hearted persons, seeing that their claim would be palpably absurd! They scorn the name as mean and paltry—unworthy of a man who loves free living and counts religion _cant_.   hypocrisy

But should there be one of you so entirely deceived by the evil spirit as to think yourself a partaker in the promises, while you are living in the lusts of the flesh, let me solemnly warn you of your error! He who sincerely repents of sin will hate it and find no pleasure in it. And during the season when his heart is broken, he will loathe to detestation, the very approach of evil! The song of mirth will then be as a dirge in his ear—"As he that pours vinegar upon nitre, so is he that sings songs to a sad heart" (Prov. 25:20). If the man who makes merry with sin is broken-hearted, he must be a prince of hypocrites, for he pretends to be worse than he is! We know right well that the wounded spirit requires other cordials than this world can afford. A soul disturbed by guilt must be lulled to a peaceful rest by other music than carnal pleasures can afford. The tavern, the house of vice and the society of the profligate are no more to be endured by a contrite soul than the jostling of a crowd by a wounded man!

2. Again, we will not, for one moment, allow that a *self-righteous* man can have a broken heart. Ask him to pray and he thanks God that he is in every way correct. What need has he to weep because of the iniquity of his life, for he firmly believes himself to be well-deserving and far enough removed from guilt! He has attended his religious duties; he is exceedingly strict in the form of his devotions; or if he cares not for such things, he is at any rate quite as good as those who do! He was never in bondage to any man but can look to Heaven without a tear for his sin. Do not conceive that I am painting an imaginary case, for there are, unfortunately, too many of these proud self-exalting men. Will they be angry with me when I tell them that they are no nearer Heaven than those whom we reproved a few moments ago? Or will they not be equally moved to wrath if I were

so much as to *hint* that they need to be broken in heart for their sin? Nevertheless, such is the case, and Pharisees shall one day learn with terror that self-righteousness is hateful to God!

The Experience of a Spiritually Depressed Heart

But what is a broken heart? I say, first, that a broken heart implies *a very deep and poignant sorrow on account of sin.* A broken heart—think of that! If you could look within, and see everything going on in this great mystery called man, you would marvel at the wonders thereof. But how much more astonished would you be to see its heart, not merely divided in two, but split into atoms! You would exclaim, "What misery could have done this? What a heavy blow must have fallen here!" By nature, the heart is of one solid piece, hard as a nether millstone. But when God smites it, it is broken to pieces in deep suffering.

Some will understand me when I describe the state of the man who is feeling a sorrow for sin. In the morning he bends his knees in prayer, but he feels afraid to pray. He thinks it is blasphemy for him to venture near God's throne! And when he does pray at all, he rises with the thought—"God cannot hear me, for He hears not sinners." He goes about his business and is perhaps a little diverted. But at every interval, the same black thought rolls upon him—"*You are condemned already.*" Mark his person and appearance. A melancholy has rested upon him. At night he goes home, but there is little enjoyment for him in the household. He may smile, but his smile ill conceals the grief which lurks underneath. When again he bends the knees, he fears the shadows of the night. He dreads to be on his bed, lest it should be his tomb! And if he lies awake, he thinks of death, the second death—damnation and destruction! If he dreams, he dreams of demons and flames of Hell. He wakes, again, and almost feels the torture of which he dreamed. He wishes in the morning it were evening—and at evening it were night. "I loathe my daily food," he says. "I care for nothing for I have not Christ! I have not mercy, I have not peace." He has set off running on the road to Heaven and he puts his fingers in his ears and will hear of nothing else. Tell him of a ball or concert— it is nothing to him. He can enjoy nothing! You might put him in a heaven and it would be a hell to him! Not the chants of the redeemed, not the hallelujahs of the glorified, not the hymns of flaming cherubs would charm woe out of this man as long as he is the subject of a broken heart.

Now I do not say that all must have the same amount of suffering before they arrive at Heaven. I am speaking of some who have this especial misery of heart on account of sin. They are utterly miserable. As Bunyan has said, "They are considerably tumbled up and down in their souls"—and conceive that, "As the Lord their God lives, there is but a step between themselves and eternal death." Oh, blessings on the Lord forever! If any of you are in that condition, here is the mercy. Though this wound is not provided for in any earthly pharmacy—though there are found no physicians who can heal it, yet, "He heals the broken in heart and binds up their wounds" (Ps. 147:3). It is a blessing to have a broken heart, after all!

Again—when a man has a broken heart, he not only feels sorrow for sin, but he feels himself *utterly unable to get rid of it.* He who believes himself able to save himself, has never known the meaning of a broken heart. Those who imagine that reformation can atone for the past—or secure righteousness for the future—are not yet savingly brought to know them. No, my friends, we must be humbled in the dust and made to look for all in Christ, or else we shall be deceived, after all! But are you driven out of yourself? Are you like the wounded soldier crying for someone else to carry you to the hospital of mercy and longing for the aid of a mightier than yourself? Then be of good cheer, there shall be found a great deliverance for you! So long as you trust in ceremonies, prayers or good works, you shall not find eternal grace. But when stripped of all strength and power, you shall gain a glorious salvation in the Lord Jesus! If morality can join the pieces of a broken heart, the cement shall soon cease to bind and the man shall again be as vile as ever. We must have a *new heart* and a right spirit, or vain will be all our hopes!

Need I give any other description of the character I desire to comfort? I trust you are discovered. Oh, my poor brothers and sisters, I grieve to see you in distress, but there is pardon through Jesus—there is forgiveness even for you! What? Though your sins lie like a millstone on your shoulders, they shall not sink you down to Hell! Arise! He, my gracious Lord, calls you! Throw yourself at His feet and lose your griefs in His loving and cheering words! You are saved if you can say—

"A guilty, weak and helpless worm
On [Christ's] kind arms I fall.
[He is] my strength and righteousness,
My Jesus and my all."[2]

---

2. Isaac Watts, *Hymns and Spiritual Songs,* Hymn 2:90 Stanza 6: "Faith in Christ for Pardon and Sanctification." http://www.fullbooks.com/ Hymns-and-Spiritual-Songs5.html.

The Mercy of God for the Broken Hearted

We have spoken a long time on the great ill of a broken heart. Our second thought will be the great mercy—"He *heals* the broken in heart."

First, *He, only*, can do it. Men may alleviate suffering, they may console the afflicted and cheer the distressed, but they cannot heal the broken in heart, nor bind up their wounds! It is not human eloquence, or mortal wisdom. It is not the oration of an Apollos, nor the wondrous words of a prince of preachers. It is the "still small voice" (1 Kings 19:12) of God which alone confers the "peace which passes all understanding" (Phil. 4:7). The binding of the heart is a thing done immediately by God, oftentimes without any instrumentality whatever!

But when instrumentality is used, it is always in such a way that the man does not extol the instrument, but renders grateful homage to God. In *breaking* hearts, God uses man continually—repeated fiery sermons and terrible denunciations break men's hearts. But you will bear me witness when your hearts were *healed*—only God did it! You value the minister that broke your heart. But it is not often that we ascribe the healing to any instrumentality whatever! The act of Justification is generally apart from all means—only God does it. I know not the man who uttered the words that were the means of relieving my heart—"Look unto Me and be you saved, all the ends of the earth" (Isa. 45:22). I do not remember what he said in the sermon and I am sure I do not care to know. I found Jesus then and there. And that was enough for me! When you get your wounds healed, even under a minister, it seems as if it were not the minister who spoke. You never heard him speak like it in all your life before. You say, "I have often heard him with pleasure, but he has outdone himself. *Before,* he spoke to my ears, but *now* to my heart." We are, some of us, rejoicing in the liberty of Christ and walking in all the joy of the Spirit. But it is to God we owe our deliverance and we are grateful neither to man nor book, so much as to the great Physician who has taken pity on us. Oh that Jesus would walk through this Bethesda now! Oh, poor sick, dying man, does guilt weigh heavy on your soul? Turn not to any helper but to Him that sits on the throne!

Then He only can do it. I defy any of my brothers to bind up a broken heart. I have often labored to do it, but could never effect it. I have said a word to console the mourner, but I have felt that I have done but little, or have, perhaps, put the wrong mixture in the cup. Only HE can do it! Some of you seek mercy through Baptism, or the Lord's Supper, or regular attendance at the house of prayer. Some of you, again, have certain forms and observances to which you attach saving value. As the Lord lives, NONE of these things bind up the broken in heart apart from the Holy Spirit! They are empty wind and air. You may have them and be lost! You can have no peace and comfort unless you have immediate dealings with God, who alone, as the great Physician, heals the broken in heart! Ah, there are some of you who go to your ministers with broken hearts and say, "What shall I do?" I have heard of a preacher who told his anxious hearer, "You are getting melancholy; you had better go to such-and-such a place of amusement. You are getting too dreary and melancholy by half." Oh, to think of a nurse in a hospital administering poison, when she ought to be giving the true medicine! If he deserves to be hung, who mixes poison with his drugs, how much more guilty is that man who tells a soul to seek for happiness where there is none—who sends it to a carnal world for joy when there is no joy to be found except in God?

Then again, God only *may* do it. Suppose we could heal your broken heart? It would be good for nothing. I do beseech the Lord that I may never get a broken heart healed, except it is by God. A truly convinced sinner will always rather keep his heart broken than have it healed wrongly. I ask you who are suffering whether you would not rather keep your broken heart as it is than allow a bad physician to cure it for you, and so deceive you and send you to Hell, at last? I know your cry is, "Lord, let me know the worst of my case. Use the knife. Do not be afraid of hurting me! Let me feel it all. Cut the proud flesh away rather than let it remain." But there are not a few who get their wounds glossed over by some pretended good works or duties. Oh, my hearer let no man deceive you! Be not content with a name to live while you are really dead. Bad money may pass on earth, but genuine gold, alone, will be received in Heaven. Can you abide the fire?

In vain your presumption! When God shall come to examine you, you will not pass muster unless you have had a real healing from His hand! It is easy enough to get religious notions and fancy you are safe, but a real saving work is the work of God and God, alone! Seek not to the priest—he may console—but it is by deluding you! Seek not to your own self—you may soothe yourself into the sleep of Hell! See that your heart is washed in the blood of Jesus. Be careful that the Holy Spirit has His temple in it and may God, of His great and sovereign grace, look to you that you deceive not yourself!

The Promises of God for the Broken Hearted

But next, God *will* do it. That is a sweet thought. "He heals the broken in heart" (Ps. 147:3). He WILL do it! Nobody else can, nobody else may, but He will! Is your heart broken? He WILL heal it, He is sure to heal it, for it is written—and it can never be altered, for what was true 3,000 years ago, is true now— "He heals the broken in heart" (Ps. 147:3). Did Saul of Tarsus rejoice after three days of blindness? Yes, and you, also, shall be delivered! Oh, it is a theme for eternal gratitude that the same God who, in His loftiness and omnipotence stooped down in olden times to soothe, cherish, relieve and bless the mourner, is even now taking His journeys of mercy among the penitent sons of men! Oh, I beseech Him to come where you are sitting and put His hand inside your soul—and if He finds, there, a broken heart, to bind it up! Poor sinner, breathe your wish to Him, let your sigh come before Him, for, "He heals the broken in heart." There you lie wounded on the plain. "Is there no physician?" you cry! "Is there none?" Around you are your fellow sufferers, but they are as helpless as yourself. Your mournful cry comes back without an answer and space, alone, hears your groan. Ah, the battlefield of sin has one kind Visitor. It is not abandoned to the vultures of remorse and despair. I hear footsteps approaching! They are the gentle footsteps of Jehovah! With a heart full of mercy, He is hastening to His repenting child. In His hands there is no thunder, in His eyes no anger, on His lips no threat—look how He bows Himself over the mangled heart! Hear how He speaks, "Come, now, and let us reason together, says the Lord; though your sins are as scarlet, they shall be as white as snow; though they are red like crimson, they shall be as wool" (Isa. 1:18). And if the patient dreads to look in the face of the mighty Being who addresses him, the same loving mouth whispers, "I, even I, am He that blots out your transgressions for My name's sake" (Isa. 43:25). Look how He washes every wound with sacred water from the side of Jesus! Mark how He spreads the ointment of forgiving grace and binds around each wound the fair white linen, which is the righteousness of saints. Does the mourner faint under the operation? He puts a cordial to his lips, exclaiming, "I have loved you with an everlasting love" (Jer. 31:3). Yes, it is true—most true—neither dream nor fiction, "He heals the broken in heart and binds up their wounds" (Ps. 147:3).

God's Kind and Humble Strength

How *condescending* is the Lord of Heaven, to thus visit poor forlorn man! The Queen has kindly visited the hospitals of our soldiers to cheer, by her royal words, her loyal defenders. By this she has done herself honor, and her soldiers love her for it. But when the God of the whole earth, the Infinite Creator, stoops to become servant to His creatures—can you conceive the majestic condescension which bows itself in mercy over the miserable heart and with loving fingers closes the gaping wounds of the spirit? Oh, sin-sick sinner! The King of Heaven will not despise *you*, but you, too, shall find Him your Comforter, who heals all your diseases! Mark, moreover, how tenderly He does it. You remember that passage in the Psalms, "Loving-kindness and *tender* mercies" (Ps. 103:4)? God's mercies are "tender mercies." When He undertakes to bind up the broken in heart, He always uses the softest liniment. He is not like your army surgeon who hurries along and says, "A leg off here, an arm off there." But He comes gently and sympathizing; He does not use roughness with us; But with downy fingers He puts the wound together, and lays the plaster on. Yes, He does it in such a soft and winning way that we are full of wonder to think He could be so kind to such unworthy ones!

Then He does it *securely*, so that the wound cannot open again. If He puts on His plaster, it is Heaven's court plaster and it never fails. If He heals, He heals effectually. No man who is once saved of God shall ever be lost! If we receive mercy by faith, we shall never lose it. When God heals once, He heals forever! Although some who teach false doctrine do assert that children of God may be lost, they have no warrant in Scripture, nor in experience, for we know that He keeps the saints. He who is once forgiven cannot be punished. He who is once regenerated cannot perish. He who is once healed shall never find his soul sick unto death. Blessings on His name—some of us have felt His skill and have known His mighty power! And were our hearts broken, now, we would not stop a moment, but go at once to His feet and we would cry, "O, You who bind the broken in heart, bind ours! You who heals wounds, heal ours, we beseech You."

A Hard Word for the Hard Hearted

And now, my hearers, a parting word with you. Are you careless and ungodly? Permit me to speak with you. Is it true that after death there is a judgment? Do you believe that when *you* die, *you* will be called to stand before the bar of God? Do you know that there is a Hell of eternal flame appointed for the wicked? Yes—you know and believe all this—and yet you are going down to Hell thoughtless and unconcerned—you are living in constant and fearful jeopardy of Hell's fires—without a friend on the other side the grave! Ah, how changed will your note be soon, you have turned away from rebuke, you have laughed at warning, but laughter will then give place to sighs, and your singing to yells of agony! Think about it, my brothers and sisters, before you again place your life in peril. What will you do if your soul is required of you? Can you endure the terrors of the Almighty? Can you dwell in everlasting burnings? Were your bones of iron, and your ribs of brass, the sight of the coming judgment would make you tremble! Forbear then to mock at religion. Cease to blaspheme your Maker, for remember, you will soon meet Him face to face—and how will you then account for your insults heaped upon His patient person? May the Lord yet humble you before Him!

A Kind Word to the Soft Hearted

But I am seeking the distressed and I am impatient to be the means of his comfort. It may be my words are now sounding in the ears of one of my weary, wounded fellow countrymen. You have been a long time tossing on the bed of languishing and the time for thought has been blessed to your soul by God. You are now feeling the guilt of your life and are lamenting the sins of your conduct. You fear there is no hope of pardon, no prospect of forgiveness—and you tremble lest death should lead your guilty soul unforgiven before its Maker. Hear, then, the word of God! Your pains for sins are God's work in your soul! He wounded you that you may seek Him. He would not have showed you your sin if He did not intend to pardon you! You are now a sinner and Jesus came to save sinners—therefore He came to save you! Yes, He is saving you now! These strivings of soul are the work of His mercy. There is love in every blow and grace in every stripe. Believe, O troubled one that He is able to save you unto the uttermost and you shall not believe in vain. Now, in the silence of your agony, look unto Him who by His stripes heals you; Jesus Christ has suffered the penalty of your sins, and has endured the wrath of God on your behalf. See yonder crucified Man on Cavalry, and mark you that those drops of blood are falling for *you*. Those nailed hands are pierced *for you*, and that opened side contains a heart within it, full of love *to you*—

> "None but Jesus! None but Jesus!
> Can do helpless sinners good."[3]

It is simple reliance on Him which saves! The Negro slave said, "Massa, I fall flat on de promise." So if you fall flat on the promise of Jesus, you shall not find Him fail you! He will bind up your heart, and make an end to the days of your mourning. We shall meet in Heaven, one day, to sing hallelujah to the condescending Lord! Till then, may the God of all grace be our helper. Amen.

> "The mighty God will not despise
> The contrite heart's plea for sacrifice;
> The deep-fetched sigh, the secret groan,
> Rises accepted to the throne!
> He meets, with tokens of His grace,
> The trembling lip, the blushing face;
> His [heart] yearn[s] when sinners pray—
> And mercy bears their sins away.

---

3. Joseph Hart, "Come Ye Sinners, Poor and Needy," *Hymns Composed on Various Subjects*, 1759.

When filled with grief, overwhelmed with shame,
He, pitying heals their broken frame—
He hears their sad complaints and spies
His image in their weeping eyes."[4]

---

4.   John Stenson, "Hymn 315: The Penitent Accepted," *The Baptists' Hymn Book; Being a Collection of Upwards of Eleven Hundred Hymns* (2nd ed. 1855).

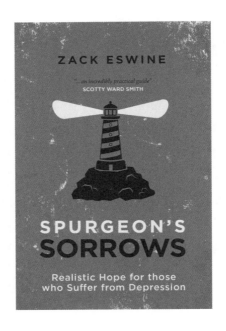

Spurgeon's Sorrows
Realistic hope for those who suffer from depression
by Zack Eswine

Christians should have the answers, shouldn't they? Depression affects many people both personally and through the ones we love. Here Zack Eswine draws from C.H. Spurgeon, 'the Prince of Preachers' experience to encourage us. What Spurgeon found in his darkness can serve as a light in our own darkness. Zack Eswine brings you here, not a self-help guide, rather 'a handwritten note of one who wishes you well.'

ISBN: 978-1-78191-538-7

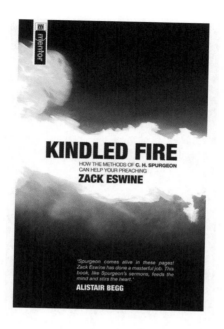

Kindled Fire
*How the methods of C.H. Spurgeon
can help your preaching*
by Zack Eswine

What would it have been like to sit in Spurgeon's classes? I hope this book gives a sense of what a student would hear Spurgeon say about preaching if Spurgeon were to speak with them in the hall, from the pulpit, or on a walk down the streets of London. Thus, the purpose of this book is to enable preachers to "apprentice" with Spurgeon for a season in order to learn from him about preaching. It is hoped that such an internship will prove valuable for contributing to preachers as they mine resources for gospel relevance and power in the twenty-first century.

ISBN: 978-1-84550-117-4

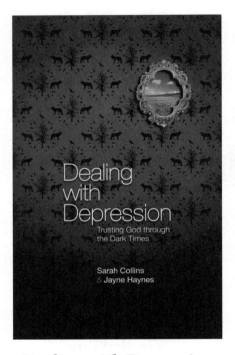

Dealing with Depression
Trusting God through the Dark Times
by Sarah Collins and Jayne Haynes

Depression is a common complaint in the doctor's surgery and 1 in 5 of the population that is 20 per cent of people will have at least one major episode in their lifetime. We are reassured here that just like our physical health we can go through good and bad emotional health. But how does the Christian deal with this? It is so easy for us to be riddled with guilt but in this book the Christian is reassured that God knows and deals with us by grace, He helps us move from guilt to grace. Written from a biblical and medical perspective.

ISBN: 978-1-84550-633-9

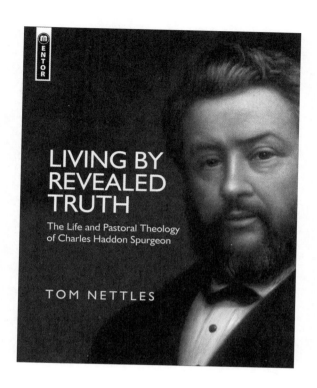

Living by Revealed Truth
The Life and Pastoral Theology of Charles Haddon Spurgeon
by Tom Nettles

Tom Nettles has spent more than fifteen years working on this magisterial biography of Charles Haddon Spurgeon, the famous nineteenth century preacher and writer. More than merely a biography it covers his life, ministry and also provides an indepth survey of his theology.

ISBN: 978-1-78191-122-8

No Tears in Heaven
by C.H. Spurgeon

No Tears in Heaven speaks of the great joy of the Christian Faith – Heaven. This book brings together, in a new way, a number of Charles Haddon Spurgeon's exhilarating teachings on Heaven. The writings of Spurgeon, in his typically beautiful and penetrating style, will deepen our anticipation of Heaven and challenge us to a closer walk with God.

ISBN: 978-1-78191-404-5

The Soul Winner
Advice on Effective Evangelism
by C.H. Spurgeon

Spurgeon was one of the most effective evangelists of all time.
Under his ministry Victorian London saw revival on a scale
never seen since. Yet Spurgeon would be the first to point your
finger away from himself to the true author of repentance and
reformation - he realised that without God at work, he could
do nothing. Here is a collection of his lectures and talks to
take people away from human inspired gimmickry and slavish
mimicry to think through for themselves how to enable God to
work in their lives and ministry.

ISBN: 978-1-87167-695-2

Christian Focus Publications

Our mission statement –

STAYING FAITHFUL
In dependence upon God we seek to impact the world
through literature faithful to His infallible Word, the Bible.
Our aim is to ensure that the Lord Jesus Christ is presented
as the only hope to obtain forgiveness of sin, live a useful life
and look forward to heaven with Him.

Our books are published in four imprints:

CHRISTIAN
FOCUS

Popular works including biographies, commentaries, basic doctrine and Christian living.

CHRISTIAN
HERITAGE

Books representing some of
the best material from the rich
heritage of the church.

MENTOR

Books written at a level suitable
for Bible College and seminary
students, pastors, and other serious readers. The imprint includes
commentaries, doctrinal studies,
examination of current issues and
church history.

CF4•K

Children's books for quality Bible
teaching and for all age groups:
Sunday school curriculum, puzzle
and activity books; personal and family devotional titles, biographies and
inspirational stories – because you are
never too young to know Jesus!

Christian Focus Publications Ltd,
Geanies House, Fearn, Ross-shire,
IV20 1TW, Scotland, United Kingdom.
www.christianfocus.com